Advance praise for *Those People: The True Character of the Homeless*

"Rich has been a constant inspiration and example for my life and the lives of so many others. The words written in this book are a message of humbleness and an inexplicable desire to be used by God. It is here, within these pages, that Rich challenges the church and its occupants, to live beyond the comfortable, and instead step forward with fierce courage and determination to joyfully lift up those in great need."

Adam Sidler
Associate Pastor, Grace Fellowship, Brooklyn Park, MN

"The connection of humanity is incredibly powerful—so many stories told and such a true gift to tell them. Richard effortlessly gives his time and his self to others. By taking on just one of the challenges in his new book, he creates an opportunity for us all to make a difference in the lives of 'those people' who appear to be different from us."

Jessica Sprenger
Former Manager, Catholic Charities: Higher Ground Shelter, Minneapolis, MN

"If you care, you will share. That simple statement is a living example of how Richard Bahr has made a difference in so many people's lives. Richard gives us life examples of how each of us in simple ways can make a difference in another person's life. Each of us are 'those people.' Some of us have a place to live and food to eat, but there may be a void in our life. Then there are others who have nothing materially and are internally rich. Richard is a man of faith, and he has turned his faith into action. His life experiences have given us many examples of how we can go out and help those in need. He challenges and motivates all of us in our own way to reach out to others to help make a difference in their lives."

Andy Zucaro
Deacon, Church of the Presentation, Upper Saddle River, NJ

"We pass by them every day. The homeless live among us in our communities, yet seldom do we really see them. If we are honest, our views of them have insulated us from seeing them as real people or feeling that it's really a problem we need to spend our time, treasures, or talents on. Richard Bahr is not someone who has a passing fad or some religious sense of responsibility to care for others out of duty. He has taken seriously the words of Jesus: Truly I tell you, whatever you did for one of the least of these brothers of mine, you did for me. Simply put. Reading the stories within, you will find real people who may inspire you to make a difference in the lives of people you may have just passed by."

Marlan Mincks
Pastor, Iron Ridge Church, Waukon, IA

"Richard Bahr is the right person to write this book. His intimate knowledge of people experiencing homelessness is born out of a myriad of hours of service to a segment of society that the general public would rather not see, let alone interact with. Not Richard! He has deep compassion for people, particularly those who are living with less. They are his friends, and their stories are lovingly shared with the reader. *Those People* is a warm invitation to see and walk in the shoes of people who courageously refuse to be defeated by their present circumstances. I am challenged by this book—even as one who has worked as an advocate and champion for people experiencing some of the deepest levels of poverty—to not just look away, but to really see with fresh eyes and a renewed mind the people Richard calls friends and cares so much about. May I exhibit the courage to put my faith in action as Richard Bahr has done and is still doing."

Captain Katherine Clausell
Divisional Social Services Director, The Salvation Army Northern Division

THOSE PEOPLE

THOSE PEOPLE

the true character
of the homeless

BY RICHARD BAHR

MINNEAPOLIS

THOSE PEOPLE
The True Character of the Homeless

Copyright © 2018 Threshold to New Life. All rights reserved. Except for brief quotations in critical articles or reviews, no part of this book may be reproduced in any manner without permission from the publisher. For permission go to www.richardbahr.com.

Publisher: Huff Publishing Associates, LLC. Minneapolis
www.huffpublishing.com

Scripture quotations marked (NLT) are taken from the Holy Bible, New Living Translation, copyright ©1996, 2004, 2015 by Tyndale House Foundation. Used by permission of Tyndale House Publishers, Inc., Carol Stream, Illinois 60188. All rights reserved.

Scripture quotations marked (ESV) are from the ESV® Bible (The Holy Bible, English Standard Version®), copyright © 2001 by Crossway, a publishing ministry of Good News Publishers. Used by permission. All rights reserved.

Cover and book design: Hillstrom Books, Inc.

Cover images: homeless man © iStock.com/monstArrr_; brick wall © iStock.com/Marchello74

ISBN: 978-0-9908073-9-1

www.threshold2newlife.org

To my friends who live in the homeless community:

You have taught me things that really matter.
You will always have a home in my heart.

CONTENTS

1. Opening 1
2. Don't pray for this (patience) 9
3. What's the attitude? (gratitude) 21
4. True grit (perseverance) 37
5. More powerful than a locomotive (stamina) 51
6. You've got to have . . . (faith) 65
7. The heart of the matter (serving) 81
8. Don't bring me down (not defined by circumstances) . . 97
9. It's better to give (generosity) 111
10. The greatest of these (love) 127
11. Conclusion 141

Acknowledgments 145
Appendix: Thoughts on dealing with panhandlers 149
Notes 157
About Threshold to New Life 160
About the author 162

CHAPTER ONE

OPENING

You stop at an intersection. Red light. You turn slightly to your right and notice a new, late model luxury car immediately next to you. Peering inside, you note a well-groomed man, clean-shaven, wearing a dress shirt and a tie, the jacket neatly hanging immediately behind him in the rear of the car. He's talking on a mobile phone, the new one you just saw on a commercial over the weekend. This guy really has it together. Probably has a big, fancy house to match the automobile. You're guessing he's of above-average intelligence, college educated, and married to a beautiful woman or has an attractive girlfriend. You figure he makes a lot of money and has a big job, probably in a leadership position at a successful company or as the top salesperson. You size him up, much of this subconsciously, in a few, brief moments.

At the next traffic light, on your left-hand side, is a man holding a cardboard sign. You glance briefly out of the corner of your left eye. You don't want to make eye contact that could create an invitation for the man to stop at your vehicle. Then you'd be confronted with the decision either to roll down your window and give him a few dollars—and we all know what panhandlers do with the money—or just stare straight ahead hoping he'll get the clue that you're not an easy mark and move to the car behind you. From the brief glance, you see an unshaven, middle-age man with unkempt hair who appears to be days from his last shower. His clothes are crinkled and his face is hardened by the weather, probably from spending so much time outside working his hustle at various intersections. Naturally you can't smell his breath, but if you could, you'd note the smell of hard liquor either from breakfast or possibly the leftover stench from partying the night before. This guy needs a job to pull himself up by his own bootstraps; after all, you're on your way to work. Why is it that you should have to feel guilty about not subsidizing this guy's bad habits and irresponsible choices? Life is what you make of it. And this guy isn't making much of his. His fault—not yours.

We all do this. We size people up, judging the book by its cover. It is arguable that there is an element of judging or discerning people and their circumstances that can be healthy and reasonable. When interviewing someone for a job opening, the interviewer is placed in this position. The interviewer's observations and determinations about the candidate, hopefully on merit-based criteria, are valuable to the organization that depends on his or her use of good judgment. We observe the friends that our children hang out with, hoping that these are "good kids" that won't lead ours astray. We make judgments about whom we desire to emulate or mentor us, typically someone that we aspire to be more like. There are many instances where the use of our judgment about others is well placed and useful. And other places it is not.

How about the man in the fancy car? What if you knew his whole backstory? That he has a serious cocaine addiction, physically abuses his wife, and as the CFO of his company he's embezzled a six-figure sum to feed his chemical addiction. On first glance, is that how this guy would appear to you? However, knowing more about him, you naturally feel much differently about him, and there's certainly no admiration for him, perhaps even distain.

What about the homeless guy flying the sign at the corner? How differently would you feel about him if you knew he was a veteran of the Gulf War, had done four tours of duty, was awarded several medals due to his battlefield bravery, and once reentered a firefight to pull out a fellow soldier who had his leg blown off by an IED? He suffers from PTSD that manifests itself by causing night terrors. He vows to stay off drugs and alcohol because he knows those aren't long-term solutions. The psychologist at the VA hospital has encouraged him to abstain from chemicals, so he only drinks on Friday nights (which he looks forward to) so on Saturday night he can rest well, and if he does, attend church on Sunday.

Both circumstances outlined above are fictitious, but neither is far from truth or reality. What we observe and what we determine or judge at the start may be radically altered by the further information we obtain. First appearances may indeed be much different than the actual reality.

As of this writing, I have worked with the homeless community for ten years. In this time I have been learning how judgmental I have been and how judgmental I can still be.

After a couple of years working a daily breakfast at a homeless shelter, I thought it would be helpful to run a coat drive and hand out warm clothing items out of the back of my truck one morning. I solicited friends, family, and coworkers to give me warm jackets, hats, and gloves that were in good condition. I also spent some of my money at local thrift shops and searched for items in good condition for the upcoming give-a-way. By the day of the event, I had about thirty warm jackets in sizes from medium to triple X. I had the foresight to presort the jackets by size so I could efficiently fill the orders—I imagined folks would line up behind my truck and allow me to wait on them one by one.

THOSE PEOPLE

When I pulled up to the shelter, I hopped out of my truck and opened the hatch. Within a few minutes, a man stopped and asked what I was doing. I explained that I had warm coats, hats, and gloves to be given to those who needed them. He asked if he could have a look at what I had. I looked him over carefully as he was already wearing all the items I had to give, and they appeared to be in good condition. I begrudgingly agreed. We sorted through my truck, and I gave him a jacket, hat, and gloves. Hmm.

This first guy nosing through the back of my vehicle seemed to attract attention. Now there were about eight to ten men all around me trying to reach in to see what I had to offer. I politely asked the guys to step back and allow me to help them one at a time. I assured them I had enough for all of them. The crowd graciously complied. After fulfilling the first few orders, the next man stepped up and asked for an extra-large-size jacket. I quickly handed him one, as I knew exactly where each jacket size was located. He examined the jacket, looked at me, and said, "You have anything else?" I was floored. My mind really got the best of me—I was angry. After all, I had just given the man the size he asked for. It was a clean, good condition, warm coat. There were at least a dozen other people in line behind him. What did he think this was, a department store? Perhaps he'd like to step into the changing room and try it on? Or take two or three jackets with him and pick from among them? Just who did this guy think he was?

I asked him if there was something he wanted in particular. He said, "Yes, I was hoping to get one with a hood." So I located a hooded, XL jacket for him, and he was satisfied. I was so busy with the rest of the giveaway that I didn't really process what had just happened until my drive home. Then it hit me.

I had totally judged this guy. I thought I was trying to help. I gave him the size he requested. He had a simple request that I hadn't even considered. And who am I to think that just because someone is homeless and doesn't have a permanent address that he or she doesn't have preferences? Does homelessness cause a person to no longer have a favorite color and lose all sense of style and preference including a hooded or hood-less jacket? My first thought was, "Look, pal, I just gave you the jacket size you wanted so just move along." I felt ashamed at how quickly I could discount someone else's thoughts or feelings on such a trivial matter. Here I'm supposed to be serving the homeless, and yet I disrespected this man in my own mind as quickly as one could say "hooded jacket, please."

The truth is I was that guy with the crick in my neck from trying to look at the traffic light out of my left eye so I wouldn't have to make eye contact with the guy flying the sign outside my driver's side window. Not long ago, I silently believed many of the generalizations about the homeless—that they are lazy, drug and alcohol addicted, dirty and smelly, lacking self-respect, and simply milking society for what they could get for free. I'm not suggesting that all the homeless are fine people with astounding character; however, neither are we who live more conventional lives. Someone living a homeless lifestyle does not necessarily equate with the stereotypes we have of that person. However, I do find that homeless persons have one thing in common.

I believe that homeless people and those living in significant poverty live with a sense of brokenness. These are not stupid and ignorant people. I don't say that to be offensive but to make a contrast with this statement: The homeless and poor are observant, and they live with the knowledge that many of the rest of us judge them and see them as lesser people than those who live with ample means. They know how they're viewed. And it hurts.

I've had more than one homeless person tell me how hurtful it is to spend one's entire day with people trying not to make eye contact with you. As for the rest of us, we receive eye contact often. We are looked in the eye by a family member before we leave for work, by the barista at our regular coffee shop, by our coworkers, or by the person behind the counter when we pay for our gas and pick up a gallon of milk on the way home. So imagine that every time you attempted to initiate eye contact, the other person would systematically and intentionally look away from you. What kind of a message does that send? It is cruel and harmful. It reinforces the shame that many homeless feel about themselves—that they are less than human, not an equivalent member of the race or society, undeserving of grace or love, and have no value.

A key purpose of this book is to dispel some of the common myths about the homeless. I urge you to be honest with yourself as you read this. You can feel like you're a pretty good person and that you're not one of those who is negative or judgmental about the homeless or any other segment of the population that's oppressed. If that is absolutely true, then good for you. However, in my many conversations, Q & A sessions with folks, as well as from my own experience, I find that most of us have a deeply buried sense of who "those people" are—and it's not pretty.

I wrote this book to honor some of my friends, people who have meant so much to me, have taught me so much, and have profoundly changed my life in a way I didn't expect. I can only hope to pass along some of what I have learned. These friends have taught me to slow down and get to know someone long enough to understand them, not snap to judgment so quickly, and that what appears on the surface to me might be only skin deep and not the true person. I have met people in the homeless community who have tremendous value, are intelligent, principled, charismatic, and have great character. I can only hope to achieve the character I have found in many of my homeless friends. And the more I hang with people like them, the more I learn, and the better and deeper my character grows.

The stories in this book are of real people I've come to know and love. I have changed each person's name to protect and honor his or her privacy. It's not my right to share someone's plight, which could be an embarrassment to some, without their readiness to do so.

Opening

The title of the book came to my wife, Carla, and me when we were sitting in a coffee shop when the idea for the book was hatched. It seems that "those people" can be used as a catchall for anyone not like us. The lesson buried in these pages is really about being judgmental, and how we each suffer from this to varying degrees. So "those people" might be any group upon which you place your unfair biases. The subject here is the homeless and chronically impoverished, but "those people" could be anyone or any group to which you do not belong. My caution is to be slow to judge, get close, and know them; you'll likely find out you were wrong on some, perhaps many, accounts.

My stories are filtered through the window of my faith and beliefs. For me it's impossible not to relate what I've been learning to what Scripture says and the parallels to my experiences in serving the homeless. If you don't share these beliefs, I'm hopeful you'll still find utility in this book. Please respect the fact that our clients often bring their faith into matters without any prompting on our part. It seems in communities where struggling and oppression exist, God seems to show up in tangible and meaningful ways to people. That's just how it is; we often haven't introduced any sort of faith message to our work. The clients do.

Each chapter ends with a challenge. You're called to rise to this if you wish, but the challenges serve as a way to begin a journey to live differently. I offer some practical suggestions in the hope to inspire readers to not simply take in knowledge into the head, but allow the learnings to pierce the heart.

CHAPTER TWO

DON'T PRAY FOR THIS

(patience)

"Patience is a virtue." Who hasn't heard that before?

The word *patient* is defined as "able to remain calm and not become annoyed when waiting for a long time or when dealing with problems or difficult people."[1] Notice the word *and* in the definition. That means we have to do both. We must keep our cool, not get bent out of shape while waiting for a long period of time. I can definitely keep cool in lots of situations. And I can wait for long stretches when the situation calls for it. But do both at the same time? Forget it. That's not a strength of mine. Not at all.

This virtuous characteristic of being patient was identified as something for all of humanity to aspire to and was possibly sourced back to writings from the fourteenth century.[2] It seems people have struggled with being patient for a very long time.

THOSE PEOPLE

Our culture has done little to improve the situation. As a matter of fact, we often work against the patience of people. It seems to be more virtuous to have the fastest drive-through line at your restaurant than it is to practice the art of dutiful waiting. Can you imagine a restaurant that would advertise the promise to never get you in and out in less than two hours and vow to not deliver your meal for at least thirty minutes after you've ordered? This could be the shortest grand opening in the restaurant business ever. I'm not sure who would go.

Better to be impatient

We reward the impatient. I have a business degree by education and have worked in industry in managerial roles for most of my career. I learned early on that being impatient was a good thing. By pushing, cajoling, and urging people along as though there was no time to wait, our firm would better satisfy customers with on-time deliveries, we'd get more done and therefore have more capacity for more work, and I'd make more money. We even used personality profiles when we hired management positions that tested for the lack of patience. Seems like an admirable character trait when you're in a responsible position.

That's until things go wrong. We push too hard to go too fast. Our quality slips. We ship defective product to the field. Our people are tired and stressed. They like the type of work they do but it seems we sometimes don't have time to do things as well as we'd like.

Am I suggesting that we take as much time as we'd like completely without regard to what a customer needs for the delivery of their product? Or we let workers decide how long they'd like to take to complete a task and simply ignore schedules? No, not really. I do wonder about the trade-offs between time, cost, and quality, and can see with the benefit of hindsight that I've too often been willing to put things at risk to reduce time. And the trouble is in the short term it seems to work. It's the long-term effects that can sneak up on us.

Our world has polluted the idea that patience has any value. Microwave ovens, cell phones, email, and Amazon Prime have eliminated the need to wait very long for much of anything. But those same people are supposed to wait and be patient on things such as a needed character change in life, a message from God about what to do next, or watch their kids or grandchildren move to and fro on a swing at a park. How many times have you seen families in a park or restaurant and everyone is spending more time looking at their mobile phones rather than being engaged with the people who are physically present?

Personal conversations take time, and my ability to control the conversation is limited. With the social media apps on my smartphone, I can decide whose post I read, which videos and links look interesting enough to click on, drop the link when I lose interest, and do this all at my own pace. Of course, only if the cellular coverage doesn't make me wait. Patience. We're generally just not that good at it.

My struggle

I struggle with patience. I mean *really* struggle with patience. I've never considered it to be one of my strengths. And as a matter of fact I've learned that to get ahead in life when following the world's rule, I must be impatient. Impatient people get more done.

One of the things I love about my wife is her character. She seems to move through life so effortlessly, within relationships and situations that really irk me. Not only this, but she's very astute in helping me see where I fall short. Okay, sometimes it's not really great to hear those things from her, but after I've allowed a little time for the feedback to settle in, I'm glad she told me.

One of those things is sighing. She's told me that when I'm in a situation where things seem to be dragging on and on, I sigh. I let out an exhaled breath, usually fairly quietly but noticeable to her. Breathe in, breathe out ... sigh. It happens when I just can't seem to stand how long the situation is taking. Whether it's waiting in line or in a conversation to which I'm a bystander and it goes on longer than I can tolerate, I sigh.

What's key here is how it may affect those around me if they knew that I'm impatient with them. Let's face it: we have lots of thoughts and feelings about people and situations that we never share. That's a good thing. Most of us have a filter in place so that we share with others only what's appropriate. So when I sigh, it could really put someone off, make the person feel bad, or reflect poorly on me if it were detected. So being aware of this allows me the opportunity to choose differently when I sense I'm being impatient. I can refrain from sighing.

Getting it right

When our children were still little, we decided to get a dog. I grew up with dogs, and we thought we'd like our kids to have the experience of having a pet. So Carla contacted a local animal shelter, and in short order, Toby the border collie was the newest resident in our home.

One of the challenges with Toby was that he would get carsick. That was a big problem for our lifestyle. We have a small lake cabin about an hour and one-half away from our home that we visit during the weekend from the months of April to October. An hour and one-half ride in a vehicle was too much for Toby. We consulted a veterinarian and got a prescription for anti-sickness medication but nothing worked. Toby kept getting sick during the car ride.

During one of our trips to the lake, we were on a county highway in a rural area when Toby lost it. I mean really lost it. I won't describe it in

Don't pray for this (patience)

any more detail other than you can imagine the mess. The kids were screaming and generally freaking out in the back seats of our Suburban. So I pulled over by the side of the road, all the doors flew open, and the kids jumped out of the truck. I calmly, quietly, and patiently told them to wait by the side of the road, and I'd take care of things. I cleaned out the truck as best I was able, then we got back in and continued our journey.

I mention this because I believe I'm rarely patient. When I asked Carla if there was a time that sticks out in her mind when I was patient, she brought up this story immediately. So why could I be patient in this situation and not in so many others? Perhaps it was because I placed the needs of my children and their concerns ahead of my own. Or maybe I felt bad for Toby because he couldn't make the trip without getting sick. We all know what vomiting feels like, and it's not pleasant. I think that much of impatience is based on self-centeredness. When I'm not getting my way, which includes things happening in my time, I get impatient. Rarely is there a time that impatience is based on a virtuous characteristic. It's almost always based on selfishness. And in this case, I put the needs of others ahead of my own. So I was patient.

Long time in line

In most cases, the homeless are required to wait for just about everything. As a society we seem to place little value on their lives, so we place little value on a homeless person's time. We think to ourselves, "What else do they have to do, anyway?"

If you show up outside of a homeless shelter anywhere in the country within an hour of check-in time, you'll see a line. In many cases it's a long line. And because all the bunks and sleeping situations are not quite equal to others, people will line up well in advance of the check-in time. One shelter in Minneapolis wanted to discourage the men planning to check into the shelter from hanging out near the entrance to the shelter or in lining up outside too far in advance of the check-in time. To enforce the rule, anyone caught on or near the property prior to the check-in time might not be allowed to stay there for at least that night anyway. So what do the prospective shelter residents for the evening do? They stay up the block to either side of the shelter, just out of sight of the shelter security staff. Then close to the time when it is permissible to line up at the entrance, they race to the shelter to get the best spot in line and therefore the better spots in the shelter to sleep for the night.

And what do the men do while they are up the block? They wait. There's really not much else to do but wait.

Job's patience

Having patience is a sought after and admired characteristic in Scripture. The saying, "That person has the patience of Job," is a maxim that continues to be commonly used in today's language. Job certainly had a difficult time. Imagine being the richest guy around, with a loving wife and great kids, and admired by all. Then in a single day, he lost his fortune and his children. Then his wife who stood by his side all those years said to him he'd be better off dead. When he sought comfort from his pals, their superstitions led them to believe that some sort of karma must exist, and when a person had a hidden sin, he or she got punished at some point. They blamed Job for his condition, when in fact he wasn't the cause. God doesn't operate in a quid pro quo fashion.

Job was such a righteous guy that the writer of the book of James has this to say about him: "We give great honor to those who endure under suffering. For instance, you know about Job, a man of great endurance. You can see how the Lord was kind to him at the end, for the Lord is full of tenderness and mercy" (James 5:11, NLT).

Don't pray for this (patience)

James was admiring and holding Job up to a high standard of patience hundreds of years after the events occurred. No doubt what was admired then, and now, is the incomprehensible suffering Job endured, with no support from his wife or friends, and yet he remained patient before the Lord. Well, mostly patient. Job had a lot of questions for God about his plight, but he always returned to defer and to trust all things to God. James may have used this example because in the early church there were tragic events, suffering, and sacrifice all taking place for the sake of spreading God's Good News about Jesus throughout the known world. James used the story of Job to encourage the people of his time—and the current-day reader—that if God can provide the strength and perseverance Job needed to make it, he will surely do this for others.

A journey of patience

My friend Bill is a picture of patience. He does get a bit restless about things from time to time, but I knew he is really an amazing guy when he described his journey into homelessness and how he's working to climb back out.

Bill grew up in a suburb of the Twin Cities with his nuclear family intact. After graduating from high school, he attended college and received both his undergraduate and master's degrees before the age of thirty. Although he didn't study music formally in college, he pursued this through church and became an accomplished organist and music director.

His extended family owned a small manufacturing company in which he became involved. This was right in line with his college studies so the fit seemed perfect. In short order, Bill became the general manager for the firm. After purchasing a home on a nearby lake, life seemed to be working out just great. Bill was living the American dream.

THOSE PEOPLE

Somewhere around this time, Bill began to nose around with certain family members into some family secrets about which he seemed to be the only one not in the know. I'm not clear on how he discovered the ugly truth, but it came out. Bill discovered that much of what he believed about his family, who he was, and how he was raised was a total lie. Devastation would be an understatement of Bill's feeling. He felt smothered, deceived, and alone. About this same time, Bill discovered he was suffering from an illness that he believed was brought on by environmental factors.

So Bill left. He left everything. He quit the family business, walked away from his home, and skipped town. He had to get away, sort everything out, figure out who he was, and somehow reestablish his identity. He moved into the deep southwest. The area had beautiful scenery, great hiking trails, and most of all it was far, far away from his problems. Bill didn't feel ready to work and had enough money saved up to get an apartment to exist for a while. He became involved in a church in the area, with music being the gateway, while he worked on himself. The apartment he scored had a dynamite view. This was some good therapy, he thought.

Then the money ran out. Unable to work due to not having recovered from the trauma, he lost the apartment and all that went with it. Penniless and able to carry all that he owned, he returned, begrudgingly, to the Twin Cities. He entered the shelter system in St. Paul where he met a man who worked there who had a calm demeanor and a good ear for listening. This fellow helped Bill a lot, not necessarily because of what he said, but through what he did. He listened. Bill really needed someone to talk to. He tried professional help on a few occasions, but felt like he wasn't getting anywhere and wasn't understood. Bill possesses a strong faith in Jesus, so when the therapy he received didn't come from that place, he felt it was ineffective.

The shelter also put him to work. As a regular at this shelter, one could volunteer for certain jobs to help out, like mopping floors,

Don't pray for this (patience)

wiping down the sleeping mats, or the like. Bill enjoyed having something constructive to do, and it came with certain privileges like the ability to come into the shelter early. In Minnesota during the winter, that was a real perk.

I'm not sure what happened, but that time came to an end and Bill moved over to the Minneapolis shelter system. That's where we met. He was a regular at our morning breakfast. He was such an intelligent guy, quick to smile and laugh, a deep thinker, and always courteous, so I enjoyed the opportunity to connect with him during my serving days. He and I spent several years meeting up at the morning breakfast until the shelter he was in decided he had been there too long. Since he was now eligible for Social Security, the staff at the shelter felt he should move on to another shelter where he could connect with an advocate who would help him apply for his benefits and find suitable housing.

I found this out when I ran across Bill in a sleeping bunk at another shelter I frequent. I was really surprised to see him in a different context. He explained the previous shelter had asked him to move; he was applying for Social Security and looking for housing. These were the biggest steps forward I had seen Bill take the entire time I knew him. He began collecting his benefits, worked with his advocate to search for and locate a nice apartment, and as of this writing, he is on the waiting list for an apartment, a process that normally takes at least six months.

The entire journey from finding out the family secret, the environmentally induced illness, his time in the southwest, being homeless, and finally waiting on a list for an apartment had taken more than fifteen years. Each time I saw Bill during those years, I would always begin my greeting with, "How are you, Bill?" No different than how most of us greet others. Except, based on the relationship I have with Bill, he knew differently. This wasn't your customary salutation; rather, it was a sincere question, and one that he always answered. He'd begin with a smile and a chuckle. But the laugh may have been intended to hide the pain of the past week. Bill would spend day after day wandering the streets of the city, sitting alone on park benches, looking up things in the library, and more importantly, praying to God all in an effort to sort out for himself the events of his past and to work out how to move forward. This was a long journey, but it was Bill's journey, one which he had the patience to travel so that he could find how he could become restored to the man he believed God intended him to be.

Enduring patience

Here's another take on patience. The author of Hebrews has this to say: "Therefore, since we are surrounded by such a huge crowd of witnesses to the life of faith, let us strip off every weight that slows us down, especially the sin that so easily trips us up. And let us run with <u>endurance</u> the race God has set before us. We do this by keeping our eyes on Jesus, the champion who initiates and perfects our faith. Because of the joy awaiting him, he endured the cross, disregarding its shame. Now he is seated in the place of honor beside God's throne" (12:1–2, NLT).

I underlined the word *endurance* to point out that in other versions of this text, the words *perseverance* and *patience* are also used. The Greek word in the manuscript from which this was translated is *hupomone*, which can mean all of those things.[3] *Hupomone* can also mean steadfastness, consistency, and endurance. The author of Hebrews is using the metaphor of running a race, and if you're going to win, there are certain things you need to do.

First, strip off every weight. Can you imagine a runner carrying weights or a forty-pound bag of salt while running? No doubt that would make anyone slower. This is compared to sin in our life or the parts of our life that need cleansing, renewing, or just plain removal.

Don't pray for this (patience)

Next, run the race with endurance, patience, and perseverance. We're to stay within the boundaries of the course and just keep going. I have several friends who run marathons (not me, I don't get the appeal) and they describe hitting "the wall" about the twentieth mile. It takes a lot of effort, not just physical effort but the battle of the mind to push through the invisible barrier. This provides an example of following God and his will in our lives. That may mean we are confronted with some real challenges, things we don't necessarily want to do. Or we may even find that things are mundane or flat for a period of time in our lives. I know of people who have described that time like a "spiritual desert," which would be like hitting mile marker twenty in your life. What is our response? Push through, keep going, and don't stop.

Finally, we keep our eyes on the prize. Runners imagine the finish line, what it will be like to finally get to the end. And competitive racers visualize what their experience will be while on the podium, leaning down to have the winner's medal placed over their head and around their neck. Jesus is our prize, in this life and for eternity. We depend on and owe everything to him.

Bill embodies these traits described in the Hebrews verses—to have the perseverance to push through after learning the devastating news about himself and his family. He endured more than a decade and a half of being mostly alone, away from home, and ultimately without a home at all in search of meaning for himself. That was how he could move forward. And to have the endurance, like a marathoner without knowing where the finish line is, Bill kept running. He continued on day after day and figured out how to meet his basic needs while running the race of his life with no end in sight. I'm thankful for the man at the shelter in St. Paul who took time to know Bill and listen to him when he was at his low point. Bill must have felt as if he were receiving a drink of cold water during a long-distance race.

THOSE PEOPLE

I admire Bill for his patience and endurance as well as his courage. Some people might have thrown in the towel and given up on life, or turned to alternative means to forget about the problem like with alcohol or drugs. Bill didn't do any of those things. I honestly don't understand all the decisions Bill made and why he gave up on professional help so early on in the process. There's no way to determine if that was a right choice or not. I do know that he's my friend, and I love his great character.

Bill embodies *hupomone* to me.

          ◆   ◆   ◆

CHALLENGE Next time you're in a situation in which you can feel your blood pressure rising due to being inconvenienced and experiencing a lack of patience, slow down and ask yourself: What would God have me do with this extra time he's given to me right now?

CHAPTER THREE

WHAT'S THE ATTITUDE?

(gratitude)

Gratitude is a virtue that we should all have. Some have it more than others, and yet certain people seem to have little of it at all. It's easy to think how grateful one would be *if* certain things would occur, like winning the lottery or finding out that one's cancer has gone into remission. We figure we would be grateful if we had someone else's good fortune, such as the rich and famous. However, a short study of celebrities reveals that those in the public eye often act entitled and bratty, not grateful in the slightest for what they have. In the end, the rate of suicide among the wealthy is higher than those with less income.[1] So if people considered wealthy are actually grateful for what they have, why are they so depressed and in a seemingly endless pursuit of further pleasure? And would we act any differently in those circumstances? Honestly?

THOSE PEOPLE

It is becoming more widely accepted that people can increase their level of gratitude, which then will positively affect their overall well-being and happiness. Even beyond this, the positive physiological effects of having a good attitude, which would include gratefulness, is widely accepted. The magazine *Psychology Today* states in an online post that "Gratitude is an emotion expressing appreciation for what one has—as opposed to, for example, a consumer-driven emphasis on what one wants. Gratitude is getting a great deal of attention as a facet of positive psychology. Studies show that we can deliberately cultivate gratitude, and can increase our well-being and happiness by doing so."[2]

In my early days in recovery meetings to deal with my addictions to drugs and alcohol, I was often counseled and encouraged by those older and more experienced than me. I was pretty young when I first began working on my recovery, so most people in the meetings were older and wiser. As I struggled with issues of temptation, friendships, family, girlfriends, money, or you name it, I remember being told to adopt an "attitude of gratitude." Since these words rhyme, they create a catchy little phrase. But what does it really mean, and how exactly are we to be grateful? Isn't that the central issue for most of us? Too often we need to have an object with which we associate our gratitude. We need to attribute it to a promotion at work, the birth of a first child, the acceptance of a marriage proposal, or a surprise of breakfast in bed provided by our children on our birthday. On the uncommon occasions when these events happen, we easily find our attitude of gratitude due to the special, unique, and explicitly positive event that just occurred. Even the person with a sour disposition in life may smile in such circumstances. I'm not saying those times don't count on the gratitude scorecard for life, but let's face it, those situations are easy.

Apostolic attitude

The apostle Paul provides a great role model for gratitude. He was a man who was imprisoned, beaten, stoned, shipwrecked, whipped, and starved, yet in and through it all, he was able to make the following claim about his own life and attitude: "Not that I was ever in need, for I have learned how to be content with whatever I have. I know how to live on almost nothing or with everything. I have learned the secret of living in every situation, whether it is with a full stomach or empty, with plenty or little" (Philippians 4:11–12, NLT).

In his letter to the Philippians, Paul says that in whatever situation he was in, he learned "to be content." To me this implies that contentment may not be an automatic response to the situation, but that we are to *be* content. Even in the first century it was believed that we could directly affect our attitude, contentment, and gratitude. Paul's attitude was not affected by his circumstance. This means that when things are going well, we are not to take undue credit and feather our ego with the goodness we have in the moment. And as well, we are not to remain in the doldrums when we struggle with life's challenges.

In addition, Paul says he's learned the secret of how to face whatever hand he's dealt. Paul continues, "For I can do everything through Christ, who gives me strength" (v. 13). He credits Christ (Jesus) for providing the strength needed to persevere in any situation. One could argue that people who follow Jesus don't always adopt Paul's attitude. True. I know a number, too many, people who would claim to be Christians and have chronically poor attitudes. Could that be a testament to the genuineness of their faith? Not for me to say, but it does beg this as an obvious question. And just as well, there are people that have no stated faith in a higher being or specifically Jesus, and yet these folks have good attitudes in tough circumstances. I really do think that is an admirable and curious thing. It is certainly possible to have an attitude of gratitude without Jesus, but I wonder if it's easier to do this and not be alone in it, why do it alone?

THOSE PEOPLE

A holiday of thanks

In my observations of the homeless, I would say a remarkable number of people claim to have faith, and many of those expressing a faith would claim Jesus as the object of it. This is likely due to the region that I serve—in the United States and specifically in the upper Midwest—and that the faith expressed might be very different elsewhere. And I also experience many folks who live in shelters, under bridges, or are just coming through homelessness who have almost unbelievable levels of gratitude. So much so that I've spent many times driving home reflecting on my own level of gratitude, all the good things that I have going for me in my life and even experiencing some mild guilt for not possessing continuous, unflappable gratitude. It just seems that I should have a continual level of gratitude if I were to compare my life circumstances to theirs.

All of this reminds me of a message I wrote and read for our family gathering one Thanksgiving. Following is an excerpt from that message.

* * *

> It becomes a rather straightforward exercise to express one's gratitude for the temporal things in this life—food, shelter, family, friends, job, and even good health. How about contemplating for a moment the things to be grateful for over which we exercise no control?
>
> How is it that the first molecule was formed from absolutely nothing? How is that anyway? And how about the creation of the first life-giving carbon atom? And life's breath breathed into the first living creature. How is it that humans have been so significantly distinguished as unique beings from animals? How could that be? Who is responsible for that?
>
> You did not select the era in which you were born. You could have been born during one of the two world wars, been called into service, and died an early death as many did as they fought for our freedom. You could have been born a pioneer, struggling simply to stay warm and fend off disease while caring for your young family in a sod hut in the plains of North Dakota. Or how

What's the attitude? (gratitude)

about being born into a time when people were persecuted and oppressed for living out their faith when the only choice they had before them was to risk it all to leave the only place they'd ever known and climb aboard a ship bound for a wilderness that is now called America?

How about the lack of control over the place in which you were born? You could have been born in present day West Africa—Liberia, Guinea, or Sierra Leone—that has been ravaged by the Ebola virus in recent years, striking terror of likely death to those afflicted. How about being born into one of more than one hundred nations, more than half of the population of this planet, that is required to figure out how to live on two dollars or less per day? Or you could have been born into a nation involved in one of the many current world conflicts. The residents of these nations live in constant fear that they or a loved one may be at any moment plucked from their family.

But you were born here. You were born in this time. You were born in this place. You were brought into life, not by your choice, not through your own efforts. But somehow, you were given all this. By someone, you were given all this.

Is your life good? That is a serious question. What do you believe about your own life?

Sure, this life has its challenges. At some point we all face an inevitable physical death. Sorry to be so blunt, but it's true and you know it. But how about the time defined by the dash, you know, on the headstone in the graveyard. It shows both the date of birth and the date of death. On a headstone, life is defined by the dash between the numbers. How about life in the dash?

During life we experience hardships, physical ailments, and struggle; we suffer loss and heartache, financial worries, and relationship pains, to only name a few. We all experience a range of these things and more.

So let's think of the glass as half full. How about the breaks in life others provided? The occasional financial windfall of a tax return that was better than expected. The times in life you felt strong and well. Your closest friend taking time to listen to your concerns over a cup of coffee. The most beautiful sunset over a lake. A double rainbow. Fresh air to breathe. Even having the capacity and ability to receive this message right now is a gift.

In many instances, when we thank someone, by the nature of the act someone is the object of the thanks. We thank a waiter for refilling our beverage. We smile and thank someone for opening the door for us. We express gratitude and say "thank you" for those who step in the gap when we have a need that we are unable to manage on our own. In those cases, we say "thanks."

But how about in those instances when we have been given so much good over which we acknowledge we exercise no control? Who is the object of our thanks?

That's the biggest question in life. Who is the object of my thanks for all of the goodness in my life that I don't control and, to be fully honest, don't deserve. I didn't do anything to earn that goodness. If you are asking that question, you might be closer to the answer than you think.

When the apostle Paul wrote his letter to the church in Ephesus, he included this clear direction about who is the object of our gratitude over things that we don't control. He wrote, "God saved you by his grace when you believed. And you can't take credit for this; it is a gift from God. Salvation is not a reward for the good things we have done, so none of us can boast about it" (Ephesians 2:8–9, NLT).

We didn't control our origin; we don't pick the day we leave this life; and we don't control our destiny. We don't control any of this except for one thing—the decision over who is the object of our faith and about those things over which we have no control. That's the key decision and the most important decision in life.

When we contemplate all the good we have in our lives, it gets pretty tough to take credit. But someone deserves it.

* * *

Early morning graciousness

It continues to be remarkable to me when serving daily breakfast at Minneapolis's largest homeless shelter that our teams receive so many "thank you" and "God bless you" acknowledgements.

What's the attitude? (gratitude)

A typical day for the folks to whom we serve breakfast begins around 5:00 a.m. or earlier. We have several clients who sleep on the trains or buses overnight. Most times these people are having their rest constantly interrupted by the transit police. They're not allowed to sleep on public transportation in the Twin Cities. It's not technically illegal, just undesirable for those operating the trains and buses.[3] Others look for spots in a skyway entrance. Skyways are enclosed bridges on a level above the street that allow people to pass from one building to another and never set foot outside. They are rather popular for pedestrians in Minneapolis, particularly during the winter months. The skyways are closed and locked in the evening, but there are certain locations, such as an entrance to a stairway, that may remain open. Hiding out under a stairway is a common place for people who are homeless to attempt to get some rest. The use of both of these public domains as sleeping quarters commonly occurs during the inclement months from about October to April, sometimes a little earlier or later in the year. Sleeping or staying outside overnight becomes uncomfortable and even downright dangerous during those months.

Others that join us for breakfast come from the homeless shelter system, either residing at the shelter we use as the home base for our meal preparations or another shelter just a few blocks away. A shelter resident is required to line up at a prescribed time, wait until the shelter opens, and get checked in, which includes being searched for carrying weapons on one's self or in a bag, as well as "Breathalyzed" to test for consumption of alcohol. Each shelter has its own policies on whether or not someone intoxicated to a certain level is permitted entrance to the shelter. In one case, I've seen the shelter allow intoxicated residents into the shelter, but rather than assign them a bunk to sleep on, they are required to sleep on the floor on a mat in a designated area. It must be assumed that it is safer to sleep on the floor on a mat, so I suppose it's for personal safety and liability reasons. I'm glad there is a place for these folks, the ones that have indulged that day. Being assigned to the designated area to sleep each night seems

THOSE PEOPLE

like a shameful thing, but I've seen many of the same men occupy those spots night after night. It seems that shame, as powerful as it is, doesn't trump the force of alcohol and drugs. Addiction is a terrible thing.

Prior to opening for breakfast, which we serve from 5:30-6:30 a.m., our guests collect outside the doors of the homeless shelter and wait for us to begin. At other times folks are allowed inside and can wait in the lobby until 5:30 a.m. Either way, there's lots of standing and waiting required as a prerequisite to partaking of a simple meal.

Once allowed into the dining hall, folks line up, we ask for someone to say a blessing over the meal, and then we begin. The meal is simple: oatmeal, grits, cold cereal, coffee, and anything else we've recently received as a donation for distribution. During the course of serving the meal and afterwards as folks are leaving, our servers receive many kind greetings and expressions of thanks from our guests. This may seem like a simple and natural thing, but I see this as something not to be overlooked or taken for granted.

I've watched the irritation and ire rise in "regular" folks being served in restaurants and coffee shops. When the order isn't exactly right or prompt, customers will huff away as though some great wrong was just committed against them. We've been conditioned to expect what we want, how we want it, and to get it when we want it. You could say our economy and times have turned consumers into spoiled brats. And yet, we serve a simple breakfast, give our guests very few choices from our meager selection, and receive gracious thanks and praise.

It's not a small thing, this gesture of gratitude expressed by someone who one would not seem to have an abundance of this scarce thing. But it's offered freely and joyfully. I don't know that I have it in me to be grateful in these difficult and demeaning circumstances. But lots of folks I've served have this gratitude. And they have it in spades.

What's the attitude? (gratitude)

Sock my attitude

I've become known for giving out socks: new, fresh, clean socks. I estimate at the time of this writing I've given out more than twenty thousand pairs of socks to homeless people and panhandlers. I say this not to brag, but to make a point that I have a lot of experience interfacing with the simple transaction of handing someone a pair of socks and getting his or her reaction. I paid for the socks myself to start and now through the social ministry my wife and I established. Most often I give out cotton crew socks, although in the summer sometimes I'll pick up some no-show socks and in the winter I'll try to get my hands on wool or other kinds of thick socks to protect the feet from the elements. A typical cost for a pair of socks is about seventy-five cents, sometimes a little more in the case of the thicker socks and less if I buy socks in bulk from an institutional supplier.

I almost always receive at least a simple "thank you," and surprisingly I get hugs, handshakes, occasional tears, and other heartfelt expressions of gratitude. Why?

Socks are a commodity. Not only are they easy to find, but socks are pretty inexpensive. Oftentimes homeless shelters will have socks available for distribution, although not always new socks, but at least freshly laundered socks. So again, why would people express such gratitude over a simple, inexpensive and easily available item?

Grateful for small stuff

During my time owning and operating a for-profit business, every year I would pick out some items that I thought our team would like and buy them (in bulk!) to package into "goody bags." Then, the last week of the fiscal year (which occurred in June), I set an appointment for each person in leadership, sat down with the person to reflect on the year, and gave him or her the bag of surprises. Now, I'll grant you, some of the positive responses were simply to be respectful and polite.

However, by the end of the conversation there was always a heartfelt appreciation for the organization and its ownership, and gratitude for what we were able to accomplish together during the year. Some years were better than others, but the gratitude was always present.

I don't want to give away the exact amount I've spent on the goody bag, but let's just say for a group of people in leadership, it would be easy for any of them to purchase all of the items entirely on their own. So, if I simply gave each person things they could easily obtain on their own, why the gratitude?

You've probably already arrived at the answer, but here are some additional thoughts.

People are moved with positive emotion when they discover that another person is expending energy on their behalf. That sounds a little clinical, but when we think about, shop for, or spend time for another, it helps that person to feel special. We have singled out that person, put some thought and effort into fulfilling a need or desire, and then given the item to the recipient. A natural reaction or response to this is gratitude. It is thankfulness for the receipt of unexpected thoughtfulness and energy spent by another only for the recipient's benefit. The exact item exchanged matters less than the thought and intent.

Many of the folks we serve our breakfast to each day could, with little effort, obtain a fresh, clean pair of cotton socks. But when socks are handed to them by someone who spent time, effort, and money to meet their needs, the recipients are naturally grateful. In spite of the circumstances, they find it important to express their gratitude to the giver.

Glad to be healed!

A quick Internet search for "Bible gratitude" shows lots of content on how we are to be grateful. True. But I already know that I'm supposed

What's the attitude? (gratitude)

to be grateful. What I want to find are examples of gratitude. Perhaps when I see an example of this, I can more easily apply it to my life. Then I read the account in the Gospel of Luke about the ten men with leprosy.

Jesus was traveling to Jerusalem and in a village along the way encountered a group of men with leprosy. Leprosy was and is still a terrible disease. Although cases are less widespread today than two thousand years ago, leprosy remains devastating to the afflicted and to his or her family and friends. The lepers called out to Jesus, which would be the common protocol of the time. It was understood that the disease could be easily passed to another person by a simple touch or any physical contact (not quite as true as they believed), so people with leprosy were often forced to live separate from all others. And when others were approaching, lepers were required to announce their condition so that they could be avoided. A humiliating life sentence.

The ten shouted out to Jesus to have mercy on them. They seemed to believe, probably based on Jesus' reputation, that he had the power to heal. Jesus instructed the ten to "Go show yourselves to the priests," (Luke 17:14, NLT), which they did, and all ten were healed. But only one returned to express his gratitude to Jesus for being healed. In an odd twist, the grateful, healed leper was a Samaritan, a person who would have been despised by the audience of the time.

One would think it would be natural to have gratitude and be willing to take the time to express it to the giver when cured of such a devastating condition. Yet nine of the ten did not bother to return. Incredible. After being relieved of this devastating disease that robbed them of nearly all social contact, only one returned to thank the one responsible. Even Jesus expressed his surprise and disappointment in this. We can learn a couple of things from this example.

First, gratitude may not naturally come to us. Sure, there are times when we *feel* grateful. But feelings aren't always what we ought to use to govern our behaviors. And thank goodness we don't always act on our feelings. The rates of infidelity and murder would probably go sky high if that were the case. We are to *be* grateful, even and especially in times when we may not feel like it, because we know the situation calls for it. There is no possible way that all of the items I gave to our leadership team members were exactly what each person wanted, but rather than act how they felt—I really don't want or need this—they chose to be grateful because it was the right thing to do in the situation.

Second, gratitude is desired by the giver. Jesus didn't need gratitude, but he seemed to want to receive it from the other nine he healed. He asked, "Didn't I heal ten men? Where are the other nine?" (Luke 17:17, NLT). When I receive the gratitude from those receiving the gifts in my office or the socks at the shelter, I am encouraged and spurred to continue to give and think of others first. When someone gives to us, we can give back by offering our thanks. It seems to be the least we can do.

Gratitude returns

When Sammy and Wendy showed up to our daily breakfast, they were both dressed nicely and gave no appearance that they were homeless. Probably one of the reasons was that they were no longer homeless. They recently had found housing, Wendy was working, and Sammy was in the process of finding a job. He even knew what type of work he was looking for and exactly where he was going to apply. Sammy was studying to be a veterinary technician until he found out that he would have to be involved in euthanizing animals. He said he just couldn't do it. So he was applying to work at the animal shelters that didn't perform the procedure.

Occasionally "alumni" appear to have breakfast with us. Most of the time, people just disappear. Without more information, I always hope for the best, and that they found housing or a job, or moved somewhere near family or friends that might be a key support system to help them get back on their feet. But this was a little different.

Sammy and Wendy went through the serving line, and once I got the chance for a break from serving, I joined them at their table. Sammy explained what they were up to and said that he and Wendy just wanted to stop by, have breakfast, and thank us for all that we had done for them. That was it. Just to stop and say thanks at 5:30 a.m. to the volunteers serving breakfast at a homeless shelter. What a sweet gesture and one that I'll never forget.

Recovery from homelessness is a difficult task. Even once established, oftentimes folks are living on the edge financially, and if anything out of the ordinary happens, the chances of returning to the streets are very high. I really hope to not see Sammy and Wendy again, for the best possible reason.

Being present can be enough

Earlier I mentioned the process of entering a homeless shelter in the evening. I have spent time "working the line" outside some of the shelters, visiting with people in a simple way to provide some humanity and encouragement to the situation. Two of the people I've met and have enjoyed visiting with are Terry and Jeff.

Terry and Jeff are a gay couple who have stayed, on and off, at one of the Minneapolis homeless shelters. That's where I met them. I'm not sure how or why we connected, but we definitely connected. Based on what they've both shared with me, alcohol had wreaked havoc in their lives, going back to their families of origin right up to the present. From what I understand of each of their personal histories, they would likely blame alcohol and its effect in their lives as paving the path to the homeless shelter system.

THOSE PEOPLE

To me, Jeff seems to have kept his drinking in check more than Terry. There have been several times I saw Jeff waiting in line alone outside the shelter without Terry. There was a several-month stretch when Terry was incarcerated for an offense, which again was due to drinking. Another time I saw Jeff, he was in line outside the shelter, speaking on the phone to a nurse at the hospital where Terry was being treated for excessive intoxication. With Jeff's permission, the next time I saw Terry I asked him about the event, of which he had no memory. I corroborated the account Jeff told him of what the nurse had said about his blood alcohol rate. It was something around .40 percent, which is five times the legal limit if one were driving a car.

One time while waiting in a hallway to get into the shelter (it was sub-zero degrees Fahrenheit outside), one guy asked me if I'd pray for him. We left the line and stepped into the lobby so I could learn more about his concerns so we could pray together. Then when I returned, Terry asked for prayer too. Terry had heartfelt concerns for himself and his desire to get clean. People that continue in the addiction cycle wrestle with a lot of shame. I try to set that aside and focus on my relationship with them, which isn't conditioned by their life's choices. I've enjoyed unconditional love from others while at some really low points in my life, so I hope to give this to others. Then I got something I totally didn't expect.

One of the last times I saw Terry and Jeff, Jeff stopped me and said, "Hey, Rich. I just wanted to say thanks." I've had lots of people thank me for things so that's not unusual. What was unusual was that when I did a quick scan of what I had done for Terry and Jeff, I couldn't come up with anything. I mean anything. I've given lots of things to folks on the street, but I couldn't think of a single thing I had given to Terry and Jeff.

I said to Jeff, "Well, you're welcome, but honestly, I don't know why you're thanking me. I mean, I haven't really done anything for you or Terry." Jeff's reply was really great, and I think it goes right to the subject of the expression of gratitude. He said that I was the only person that he or the other guys knew whom they could trust, and that I took the time to come down and visit with them. He said he appreciated that I learned people's names and gave them my time by checking in and listening when someone wanted to talk. I didn't have to give them any *thing*; what I had already given was enough.

I was floored. I wasn't being falsely modest, I just really couldn't think of how I had helped them. I understand that giving people my time, connecting with them, visiting, and praying matters. Of course it does. I just really didn't get how much. The impact we make on other people by caring, expressing our love, sharing of ourselves, and being willing to be open and available really matters. It wasn't until Jeff was willing to take the time and to care enough about me to share his thoughts in front of other guys in line that I really began to understand the impact we are able to have on others. I thank Jeff for that.

Gratitude is fuel that keeps the fire of generosity burning. We are responsible for the gratitude we give to others. Giving gratitude costs us very little compared to the impact it has on the receiver. Giving gratitude is absolutely worth it. Be sure to lavish it on others' lives every chance you get.

CHALLENGE   Think of someone in your life who may not expect you to express your gratitude and then do it. Maybe it is a phone call to a former teacher, mentor, boss, or someone from your past who helped shape you into who you are. Your gratitude will be an encouragement.

CHAPTER FOUR

TRUE GRIT

(perseverance)

No other trait captures the character of one who endures long-term homelessness as much as tenacity or perseverance. The very existence of a person living on the streets depends on this. In my home city of Minneapolis, weather conditions in the winter are notoriously frigid. Leaving the homeless shelter, typically before the sun rises and with no money in one's pocket, a person is confronted by a penetrating wind, a lack of transportation, and no place to go where he or she will be happily accepted. Sometimes a public library will become a refuge, or perhaps a fast-food restaurant provided one has a dollar to pay for a coffee that will be sipped over a two-hour span to maximize the acceptable length of stay.

Basics of homeless shelter living

Sleeping in a homeless shelter can be an unpleasant adventure with more than one hundred people crammed into too small a space, attempting to settle in for the evening on overused, vinyl mats and covered by thin blankets. With lights out typically at 10:00 p.m., security staff at the many shelters sometimes enforce inconsistent application of the rules. Music and loud conversation may continue for several hours while the smells of poor hygiene and the consumption of an overly rich diet of gassy foods permeate the air. And the reward for enduring these conditions for a night is to do it again the following evening.

Meals are another matter. I'm confident in saying that many homeless are not actually starving, as are people in many other parts of the world. Nutrition is a problem where it is difficult to receive a balanced meal, and taking a supplement (vitamin) to make up the deficit is out of the question. At the breakfast we offer in Minneapolis, we allow anyone to come in even if the person is from another shelter, has ridden the mass transit all night, or perhaps has camped out near the river or railroad tracks. It is a community breakfast. We distribute sandwiches that can be taken away for lunch or a snack. We're grateful for the sandwiches, provided by another social ministry; however, most of the time it's baloney and bread. So folks get awfully tired of eating baloney day after day. Probably starts to taste like quail or manna after a while (check out Exodus 16). The dinner meal is another matter. Some shelters offer it and others don't. Where dinner isn't offered, sometimes there are sandwiches: more baloney. Some people scramble through dumpsters, and the folks that know the good ones can actually find suitable food to eat. I know it sounds gross to those of us who have never been required to resort to such efforts, but when you combine hunger and desperation you get dumpster diving. The United States Department of Agriculture estimates that 30–40 percent of the food supply is being wasted.[1] So there is some good food in dumpsters if you know where to look.

For clothing, the homeless resort to using "clothes closets," where clothing is available for free, or shop at low-price clothing

True grit (perseverance)

establishments. Many clothes closets are operated out of church basements or in conjunction with a homeless shelter or other social service organization such as a food pantry. In my experience, the clothes closets are set up with a good purpose in mind, but are often understaffed and poorly organized. People must dig through a lot of rags to get to anything that is suitable to wear—let alone something in the correct size. The ability to do laundry is a challenge too. Laundromats are expensive when one has little or no income, and most shelters do not allow the use of their equipment as they are already tasked with washing the massive amounts of bedding and towels daily.

Housing could be its own chapter. I'll leave it at that. The amount of affordable housing is diminishing, especially in my community. An unintended dynamic of a vibrant economy is increasing real estate values, typically a good thing. However, when the value of the location of a commercial property or apartment complex rises to the point at which it becomes economically viable to raze the site and rebuild with higher rents, society ends up losing affordable housing. It's a complex problem. The net result is that the homeless and working poor have fewer options.

Healthcare is often provided for the homeless by a local hospital emergency room. We have a large hospital in the city that is the common stomping grounds for our city's homeless. I've been there a few times escorting a client to receive medical care. It must be frustrating and defeating for the hospital and its staff to see so many of the homeless and impoverished community, as I'm sure the financial model for treating them isn't as lucrative as other patients. It is a business after all; we must understand that. Actually, the quality of care is quite good at this particular hospital. But if you think you have a long wait at the doctor's office, try waiting for medical care when you're chronically poor and you're trying to get in to see someone aware of this. This is a real challenge on all sides of the transaction.

THOSE PEOPLE

College student does good

Ubadah and I met for the first time outside of the shelter where our group was serving its daily breakfast. He's a tall, slim, young man with a toothy smile. He's from a West African nation and came here while still a minor. I didn't quite comprehend his story, but it sounded like he and another close-in-age relative were expelled from the household for some reason. Ubadah was now totally on his own, which is why he came to the shelter. He was back in the Twin Cities after leaving the college he was attending out east. He claimed to have a full-ride academic scholarship, and all he needed to do was reapply and then travel back to attend school in the fall.

I've heard a number of grandiose stories from folks in homeless shelters. I don't judge these people as pathological liars, but I do think there's a bit of a self-preservation about bragging; it makes one feel a little better about oneself for a moment. Yes, some folks are habitual liars and fabricate stories about things that matter. But many folks— and not just the homeless—stretch things a bit. I'm not condoning this, simply pointing out what I see as a truth.

As I heard Ubadah's story, I was imagining that he was working up to asking for a plane ticket or the money for one. No. After we spoke a few times, Ubadah simply asked if we would reach out to the college he was previously attending and cover the twenty-five dollar application fee. He had already been in touch with the college and was prepared to complete the application; he only needed the fee to be covered. So we contacted the school and sure enough, his story checked out. Ubadah was a student in good standing, had a full-ride scholarship waiting for him, and needed to pay twenty-five dollars to reapply to the school. Wow.

So we paid the fee, and Ubadah was accepted back into school. Impressively, he never asked for plane fare; instead he got a job cleaning hotel rooms. He raised enough money for the ticket then left

True grit (perseverance)

Minneapolis. I received a picture from Ubadah a couple of years later of him at graduation. We were very proud of him and so grateful we could play a very small role in his success. But...

The next fall, Ubadah showed up at a homeless shelter that I frequent. It seemed his student visa was no longer good, and he didn't have legal standing to get a job. We had no experience with such an issue. So we worked to find someone who did. We connected Ubadah with a resource in Minneapolis that among other things provided pro bono attorneys who provided services. Ubadah met with a lawyer, completed his application, and within a couple of months received his green card.

Ubadah got an IT job, his field of preference, through an employment agency and moved into a room in a house in Minneapolis that he shares with two other professional men. We're very proud of Ubadah, and I am seriously impressed with his indomitable spirit and his "no way I'm quitting" attitude.

Persistence pays off

Ed and I usually met once a week during my visits to the shelter where he was staying. We had good conversations. Ed would ask for prayer on matters that were concerning him, and then he would complain. He complained about the system, how he was treated, and how he was never going to get out of the shelter and get his own place again. Ed readily accepted the role of victim. Although I empathized with him, I would often attempt to turn the conversation around to what was his part in the situation and what he could do. And we would then pray about the stuff that was out of his control.

Ed got a lead on a place to live that was subsidized, and with his monthly disability check he qualified as a potential resident. He was added to the waiting list. We talked about his status on the waiting list nearly every week. I encouraged Ed to be persistent, positive, and professional when he would stop in and ask the apartment staff where he stood on the list. We would continue to pray for patience and wait. He moved up to number three on the list. Then, things took a turn for what looked to be worse.

Ed had a massive heart attack and nearly died. He was hospitalized for several weeks and then placed in a nursing home to aid his recovery. The whole ordeal took several months. In the meanwhile, I called the apartment complex staff to let them know that Ed was in the hospital after experiencing a heart attack, and that he wouldn't be checking in as regularly as in the past. Naturally I asked if this had any bearing on his status on the waiting list, but I didn't receive a concrete reply. I continued to visit Ed while he was in the hospital and the nursing home until he was nearly ready to check out. I was concerned about his health and how he could possibly continue his recovery while living on the street. It was now October, and the weather was beginning to turn toward winter.

While recovering in the nursing home, someone contacted Ed to let him know that he had been moved up the list and that the nursing home would be discharging him directly to his new apartment! He was very excited, and I think relieved (as was I) that he would be able to continue his recuperation in his new place.

I told Ed I was proud of him for responding to my nagging (my term, not his) by doing a good job finding the apartment, completing the application, and remaining in touch with the manager to follow up regularly and confirm his standing. He was very negative going into the process, but by the time Ed received his keys, he was able to see how he did his part and things came together.

What about the role of my phone call to the apartment manager? Or the many prayers we lifted up in the hope of Ed getting an apartment? I can only repeat what the apostle Paul wrote long ago: "And we know that for those who love God all things work together for good, for those who are called according to his purpose" (Romans 8:28, ESV). I honestly don't know if my call had any influence on the timing of Ed getting the apartment, and I surely don't actually know the impact of our prayers. But it may be that God used, not caused, Ed's heart attack to aid in moving up on the list. Who knows? You might think I would be the one pointing this possibility out to Ed, however, it was actually Ed who pointed out this possible connection to me.

Apostolic grit

When people learn about the life of the apostle Paul, many see him as a "tough as nails" man with a dogged persistence for the cause of planting churches and introducing Jesus to a large part of the known world at the time. The accounts of Paul's hardships are the stuff of legend. For the sake of the cause, he was jailed, whipped, beaten with rods, stoned, shipwrecked, and robbed, all the while being deprived of adequate food and housing (2 Corinthians 11:23–27). But Paul adopted an other-worldly attitude about his circumstances. Knowing what he endured during his life, this seems like an almost impossible statement to be coming from such a tormented man: "I know how to live on almost nothing or with everything. I have learned the secret of living in every situation, whether it is with a full stomach or empty, with plenty or little. For I can do everything through Christ, who gives me strength" (Philippians 4:12–13, NLT).

Paul was a man with a good education and on the fast track to becoming a leader and perhaps a very powerful person in Jewish circles before Jesus entered the scene. Once he encountered Jesus and came to know that the claims Jesus made about himself were true, it seems little else mattered in his life. Paul poured his life into others, providing the opportunity for many to come to know Jesus in a deep and meaningful way.

And note the source of Paul's strength. He made no claim of his own abilities, talents, or even persistence. Regardless of his circumstances, Paul knew he could do anything through Christ who was his source of the strength required to carry out the mission.

Elsewhere in this book, I share some powerful stories of faith lived out by those who seemed to have little else. Many of the people I have encountered who have continued to persevere, survive, and in some cases thrive, have held this same belief as Paul. Their remarkable and sometimes unbelievable responses and resiliency are greatly overlooked by much of society. That's not to say these same folks don't experience discouragement; yes, indeed there is that. However, those who have built a foundation of faith always seem to quickly rebound from the pit of despair and achieve a high level of peace and contentment while redoubling the effort to forge ahead.

Time after time

Shirley and her son came to Threshold to New Life requesting assistance to move from a shelter into an apartment, to help enroll her son in a new school, and to obtain a few basic things to get restarted on living independently. She had just received a new retail job and seemed to be well on her way. Our organization became involved to assist with her current needs as well as obtain some furnishings for the new apartment. After we moved the furniture, we felt good that our mission was accomplished. Not quite.

Shirley is among a handful of clients we've had that seem to come back time and time again. We try not to judge and to take each situation on its own merit, while keeping an eye out for any patterns of dependency to which our organization might be contributing. We contrast efforts of *relief* versus those of *restoration*.[2]

Relief would be efforts centered on an immediate and imminent crisis in which those affected are in a perilous situation. Think of efforts

True grit (perseverance)

immediately following a natural disaster, such as losing one's home from a fire or malnourished children in need of clean water and food. These situations are clearly in need of a relief effort, hopefully with a restoration effort to follow. Much of charitable work today is relief-centric. It's easy to raise funds for relief by showing video clips of children starving in an impoverished nation. We also feel better about ourselves when we provide relief. During the holiday season, the social ministries in which I serve inevitably receive a glut of volunteers who want to serve others as they contemplate the blessings in their own lives, which they hope to share and give to others. I'm not vilifying those who have done so, and who have stepped up to do an occasional volunteer stint at a homeless shelter, food pantry, or the like. After all, the staple, regular, and sacrificial volunteers who make up the backbone of these programs, each began their volunteer experience with their first visit. Besides, most programs in charitable circles have insufficient help, so receiving a few more volunteers at peak times of the year is welcomed. Relief efforts are critical and vital to society—both for the givers and receivers. We cannot be satisfied that our work ends there.

Restoration work is hard; it can be long term and involve setbacks. It requires regular evaluation to determine whether sufficient progress is being made by the client and whether the tactics on behalf of the supporting organization are actually helpful. It means that the same client may return, asking for a second, third, or more assistance of some sort as he or she is in the process of becoming independent from social dependency. Organizations must walk alongside the client and not do for him or her what one can and ought to do for one's self. Success in this arena leaves the receiver with a sense of accomplishment, a renewed purpose, and a fresh outlook on his or her future life. Restoration work is messy and complicated. However, it is the true and right thing to do in many of the cases we encounter.

THOSE PEOPLE

Shirley became one of our early clients with whom we began to ask ourselves the tough questions around relief and restoration. No doubt we had already provided relief. But as she came back to us time and time again, we were concerned that a pattern was developing, one to which we did not desire to contribute. So in some sensitive conversations, we began to deny her requests, yet rather than a simple "no," we pointed Shirley to where she might be better able to receive the support she needed to bridge her continued gaps. This was painful and felt like risky strategy on our part. I can only imagine how Shirley must have felt—honestly, I don't know—but Carla and I debated, agonized, consulted our grant team, and prayed for direction.

Somehow, whenever Carla told Shirley that our organization was not willing to step in to help again, Shirley would reply, "That's okay, Miss Carla, I have faith that God will take care of us." The topic of faith demonstrated by folks we've encountered is covered elsewhere in this book, and Shirley could have appeared in that chapter as well as this one. However in Shirley's case, this wasn't a one-time incident. She came back several times asking for help to get out of a jam of some sort. Carla would always dutifully take the information, review it with the others on our team, and then deliver the news to Shirley and always receive the same, positive response. We marveled at her resilience and even discussed that we might reconsider and step back into a future need she might have if we were asked. We have little idea whether Shirley is actually managing her affairs well by our standards, but I do know that most of our clients live daily on the edge of financial crisis. When an unexpected demand occurs, such as a large car repair bill, a big medical deductible, or a death in the family requiring travel to another state, it can have long-term devastating effects and put the quality of life recently built in jeopardy. We try to balance the repeating needs of clients, evaluate their requests, watch for developing patterns, and when unsure, err on the side of grace. We must also be willing to make mistakes, which I'm sure we have.

True grit (perseverance)

We're proud of Shirley's stick-to-it-ness and resiliency. Shirley is a survivor, pouring much of herself into the life of her son, who she has been raising on her own much of his life. Our hope is for her not to experience a need that causes her to return to us for assistance, and if she does, that we have the wisdom and ability to sort out how we most effectively might help.

Small in stature

I met Steve during the early days of our breakfast ministry. Steve is a "little person," well under five feet tall. His speech is a bit unique and distinctive. One of the early times I met him, we went for coffee after I finished cleaning up after serving breakfast at the shelter, and he showed me a scrapbook of his family and heritage dating back more than one hundred years. It was well put together, and he seemed quite proud of it. He also told me he recently won a rather large prize in the Minnesota State Lottery and hoped to use some of the money to help the homeless. Yeah, I know, a "hard to believe" story alert.

As time went along, I got to know Steve better. I learned more about his family, his origins, and his background. He shared with me that he did a stint in prison in another state for some sort of stealing, which I presume was a felonious theft. Steve has a brilliant mind, almost savant-like. He can tell you the day of the week for any day you choose on the calendar in any year. He has a great mind for sports statistics and trivia. Steve is a brilliant man with a disability that seems to have been a source of trauma in his life.

We had allowed Steve to step in and help serve during our breakfast. He seemed to enjoy staying busy, restocking product that was running low during the breakfast, and doing other small but critical tasks. I also experienced his anger for the first time. He threw himself into a rage when asked about a missing item from the breakfast. He overreacted to the point where he made himself seem guilty, even if he wasn't. He threw items, cursed, and stomped away. His mood seemed to turn in an instant.

Steve was an easy target for predators. I would sometimes hear other guests of our breakfast call him by derogatory, hurtful names. Frequently I would step in and correct the person, insisting, "His name is Steve," because I wanted someone to stand up for Steve, and I didn't want that behavior to be tolerated at our event. My heart hurts when I think of spending one's life growing up being teased, picked on, and abused by others simply because of one's size, a characteristic one has no ability to change. I have imagined that the years of abuse endured by Steve have taken their toll, and his defensive response has been to lash out and retaliate in whatever way possible.

There were several of us that served on various days at the breakfast who got close to Steve. I know of one guy who brought Steve to his home and later ended up estranged from him after several heated arguments and accusations. Another brought Steve to church and to our men's Bible study only to discover Steve wandering around the church, letting himself into the office, and digging through places he cleared wasn't allowed. It seems that Steve was deeply disturbed and in need of help. However, it is impossible, or at the least extremely unlikely, that one will change unless one has determined there is a need to do so. That's why I began to take Steve out to breakfast.

For a couple of years, on most Sundays Steve and I would grab a quick fast-food breakfast after we served breakfast at the homeless shelter. My hope was to establish a relationship with Steve, gain his trust, and help guide him to different thinking. Steve always insisted on getting a ride somewhere after breakfast, so we would go either to that location or at least the general direction of his desire and choose our place for breakfast. Our conversations were frequently about professional sports: players, statistics, sports history, and trivia. Steve was a very interesting person to talk with, and I often enjoyed the conversations. Not every time, but often I would turn the conversation towards his

True grit (perseverance)

goals, how he was currently living, the choices he was making, and of course, his challenges in being honest. The last topic would frequently create a cantankerous result from Steve, yet I continued to go there. Finally, after dozens and dozens of breakfast conversations, I decided to really have it out with him.

I guess I was concerned that my attempt to develop a friendship based on common ground with Steve was not as effective as I had hoped. I worked to gain his trust, established a friendship based on common conversation topics, and even provided for some of his needs for clothing and other items he requested—including digging into my spare change dish in my truck every time he rode with me. So I took a risk. I boldly and clearly confronted Steve about his lying, his stealing, and his anger. I told him that there was part of me that understood and empathized with his plight, but that he could no longer use his disability as an excuse for wrong behavior. Steve went ballistic. That ended our breakfasts together.

I'd really like to have a happy ending to report but I don't. However, I'm not convinced the complete story has been written. Since our breakfasts ended, I have visited with Steve from time to time. Our relationship is not what it was. I think calling him out really exposed him to some stuff that he was not ready to tackle. On the occasions I see him, I try to greet him warmly, but also maintain healthy boundaries so that we don't go back to the situations that permitted him to take advantage of other breakfast team members or myself. My hope and prayer is that Steve will come to know that we love him and want the best for him, and to simply surrender to the issues he's grappling with, knowing that he has friends in place to support him. I hope we get there someday.

Steve's is a story of resilience. Yes, he has his flaws, no doubt. Living on the street and in homeless shelters when one bears such an obvious disability—a condition that leaves him completely vulnerable to every predator wanting to simply feel superior through the

THOSE PEOPLE

oppression of another and to those who see Steve as easy prey to obtain a bus token, pocket change, or whatever other meager possessions he might have at the time—has to be as though one is living in hell having done nothing to deserve the trip.

Each of these folks has my utmost respect for the endurance they demonstrate and the persistence with which each lives his or her daily life. I've had my moments when it seems all is falling apart: crisis moments, things that happen, or news received that is simply terrible. However, in my life, these have been only moments. The season moves into the next and life moves onto a new, sometimes renewed place that may be different but still can be good. My friends outlined in this chapter have experienced more than simply moments, but oftentimes seasons or even lifetimes of poverty, abuse, physical setbacks, and chronic circumstances that would cause lesser people to drown in their hopelessness. But each of these people, in their own way, has survived and in many cases begun to thrive on the heels of the challenges dealt to them. These are truly remarkable people, and I'm grateful and inspired to have witnessed the example of their lives.

ə ə ə

CHALLENGE Think of someone in your life who has endured a long-term, difficult circumstance, be it a physical disability, financial hardship, or a series of challenging setbacks. Let them know how you feel about them—your admiration for their tenacity, their courage, and their perseverance. Thank them for the example they set for you and for the inspiration they provide. Do this in person if possible.

CHAPTER FIVE

MORE POWERFUL THAN A LOCOMOTIVE

(stamina)

Having stamina, or endurance, can be as much a mental state as it is physical. When most of us think of the word *stamina*, it seems to apply best to an elite athlete, such as a long distance runner or a tri-athlete competing for a gold medal, not the sort of characteristic we draw upon in everyday life.

The amount of physical stamina we have is primarily and positively correlated with how much we have exercised or worked our body. The more we exercise, the more stamina is built up, which permits us to deal with an increasing level of fatigue or stress before we reach our breaking point. It's a cycle: work hard physically to near exhaustion, rest, and do it again. This is repeated until we gain in stamina with the reward being longer and longer periods of harder and harder physical workouts before we reach a state of fatigue. It sounds like a vicious cycle, until we consider the health benefits, which of course are numerous.

There is a close link between the physical and mental when it comes to stamina. We hear of marathon runners "hitting the wall," a term used to describe the condition in which the runner's stored energy is depleted causing a dramatic falloff in pace. This commonly occurs around the 20-mile mark of the 26.2 mile race, the standard length of a modern marathon. "The wall" is not only a physical condition but also plays on the runner's mind, urging him or her to slow down significantly or even stop running the race altogether. With the body's energy sources at a low point, the mind may also be weakened allowing defeating thoughts to dominate. The connection between body and mind is closely linked.

You may be surprised that one of the admirable characteristics of many of the homeless persons I know is the tremendous stamina many possess. To live homeless, especially over a long period of time, requires the ability to endure physical hardships, to push through acute physical pain, and all the while keep one's disposition and hope intact—again the connection between the physical and psychological. I'm not suggesting that all the folks I know who have experienced homelessness have been able to do so and maintain a cheerful disposition. However, I am startled at how many times people in the reality of suffering chronic homelessness, greet me with a smile, reach out to shake my hand, or simply ask me how I am. All this, after waiting patiently in lines outdoors and suffering from the physical challenges that the wild swings of the Minnesotan weather can dish out.

Yes indeed, I'm walking

I did an Internet search on "walking can be harmful to your health" and got no direct results. Not one. Granted, I put the search phrase in quotations because I was looking for an exact match. Otherwise any of those words appearing in an article would return a result.

More powerful than a locomotive (stamina)

Removing the quotes produced about three million results. In contrast, I searched for the exact match on "baby throws up on mom" and received thirteen hits. Naturally, removing the quotes yielded millions of results again.

Why bring this up? Because it seems that no one writes about or even believes that walking can be harmful to one's health. There are thousands of articles on the health benefits related to walking. Walking is considered a low-impact exercise causing less potential damage to joints, tendons, and muscles than its close cousin of jogging. I know this first hand as I have been a runner for much of my life. In the years since I've turned age fifty, I've struggled to keep from becoming injured due to running. I now resort to walking or "power walking" as I like to think of it, because it seems to be less harmful to my body. However, generally speaking most people would agree that walking is good for our physical bodies.

Some of the homeless I know would disagree with this conclusion.

How much walking does the average person do in a day? In its conclusion on the matter, the LSU's Pennington Biomedical Research Center determined that most of us walk fewer than 5,000 steps per day.[1] The latest mobile phone I have tracks my steps per day. Unless I am intentional and actually go out for a purposeful walk, at best so far, I average about 5,000 steps per day. I recently visited Jerusalem with a private, daylong guide through the Old City and logged 24,000 steps, a record for me. We stopped for lunch and a snack, and also stopped at various sites to take them in, but we were obviously on the move a lot. As I walked, I wondered how many steps most of my homeless friends take in a day.

Flat-footed

My friend Bill is in his sixties and has walked so much that his feet are flat. I don't know that the walking caused his feet to become flat;

however, Bill claims that he didn't have any foot issues and wore standard issue shoes before he became homeless. Now he needs a triple E-width shoe because his arches have fallen and his feet have grown wider.

Once I took him to a locally owned shoe store where I have a bit of a connection with one of the owners. This store has been marvelous in providing shoes to folks we deal with who either have very large feet or some sort of foot issue. We spent over an hour getting Bill fitted, testing various shoes until settling on a nice pair of Keens. The retail value of the shoes was about $150. We both felt grateful to the owner for being so generous and helping to meet Bill's need for a good, quality shoe.

Many of the homeless suffer from plantar fasciitis, a condition that inflames the thick band of tissue connecting the heal bone to the toes.[2] One of the key causes of this condition is wearing shoes with inadequate support. Homeless people and others who struggle economically have a couple of things working against them that causes this circumstance. Without a car, many rely on public transportation and walking to get to wherever they need to go. They also do not have the luxury of purchasing new shoes that includes a proper fitting. Combined, the situation sets up for very sore feet, with sharp, stabbing pain in the heel. These same feet are required as basic and necessary transportation to a job, to attend a church, or to travel to a place to receive a meal and get shelter for the evening.

Foot hygiene

One of the ministries I serve holds a foot-washing event on the Friday before Easter, commonly known as Good Friday. Just as Jesus washed the apostles' feet on the eve of the first Good Friday, we offer to wash feet of the homeless who are participating in the early morning breakfast our group serves.

More powerful than a locomotive (stamina)

It is a humbling—and frankly kind of gross—experience to wash another person's feet. Feet are mostly confined inside of a hot, sweaty piece of leather or synthetic fabric (a shoe) that may not have much ventilation. When feet perspire and the shoe doesn't breathe well, the moisture is trapped inside the shoe and the damp skin becomes a breeding ground for bacteria and fungi. The times I have washed feet I have been so humbled to be selected to have someone trust me with such an intimate act that even if I'm a little squeamish, I would never show it because my concern for the comfort and dignity of the client is paramount.

One year the volunteer next to me was washing the feet of a fellow who had just enjoyed our breakfast served at a homeless shelter. He agreed to have his feet washed and settled into the chair while the volunteer readied himself for the upcoming task. After the volunteer removed the man's shoes and was washing his feet in the warm, soapy water, the man pulled his foot out of the water to examine it. He reached down and grabbed it, looked at it for a moment, and then wiggled the toenail on the largest toe. It moved a bit from side to side, and then the whole toenail came off as he pulled on it. Unbelievable. I just watched a man pull off his own, fungi-infested toenail right in front of me. This didn't faze him or fortunately our volunteer, who dutifully resumed the task of completing the man's foot washing while being extra careful not to touch the nailless big toe.

It takes incredible stamina to walk and remain on one's feet for hours at a time, thousands of steps per day, walking in rain, snow, and heat, while the very thing you rely on to get around—your feet—may be causing a great deal of pain or at the least some discomfort. How many of us would like to do it, year-round in a climate like Minnesota has to offer? I feel for the struggle of the homeless, and as I consider the physical aspects of their challenges, it hurts my heart.

THOSE PEOPLE

Get in the queue

I really dislike standing in line for anything. I'm restraining myself from using the word *hate* as I think that is an expression best used sparingly for really important issues. But I am tempted to associate that feeling with waiting in line. I know I'm not alone in this. When looking for a line at the store, do you try to guess which one will deliver you to the checkout clerk fastest? Yup. Then you're just as messed up as I am. However, my desire to not wait in line has nothing to do with my physical ability to do so. It is simply due to my impatience and self-imposed importance that I think my time is worth more than everyone else's.

The homeless often stand outside and wait. To be fair about it, the shelters in our area have been opening up parts of their buildings for those waiting so that they can get out of the weather, either the scorching sun or driving rain or snow. Men are allowed to wait in the staging areas, such as a hallway or an entry, until the proper hour for the shelter to open has arrived. The lines get long, often with nearly one hundred men in line at a time. The waiting areas were not designed as such so they end up being overcrowded, which can be a source of anxiety and the occasional fight. It's hard to respect others' personal space when jammed into an overcrowded hallway.

I have been outside of shelters at times when I haven't understood why the men waiting were not let in. I don't make the rules. Standing outside in 10 degree weather with the wind blowing or in 90+ degree heat with the sun baking down is more than unpleasant—it can be dangerous to one's health. And please don't mistake my disclosure that I'm taking a position that the shelters or their staffs have done something inappropriate. There are times when I don't understand the decisions at shelters I've visited and how people have been handled, and I have been concerned and have voiced such. I'm not one to sit idly by. However, facts are facts. And I've showed up at shelters and passed out gloves and stocking caps in 10 degree temperatures,

More powerful than a locomotive (stamina)

and likewise I've handed out three hundred water bottles in an afternoon while men are in the queue waiting to get inside.

All of this pales in comparison to my attempt to reduce my time in the checkout line by a minute or two. It takes some real toughness to stand and wait, and either freeze or bake while doing so.

Manna ... from heaven?

Imagine eating the same thing every day for most of your life. That's what the Hebrew people dealt with during their forty-year exodus into the desert. After crossing through the Red Sea and escaping slavery at the hands of the Egyptian Pharaoh, the Israelite people lived in the desert for forty years prior to reaching the land promised by God.

As already mentioned, it's curious how a lack of physical stamina can play with one's mind. Weeks into their newfound freedom and after more than four hundred years of slavery and oppression, the Israelites were now a liberated people and were complaining about the lack of food. The people were turning against their leaders (Exodus 16). Their provisions had run out, and they were lamenting about how well they had eaten as slaves. Short memory! God heard the pleas of the people and provided for their physical needs by delivering quail for their meat, and manna, thought to be a wafer-like substance that had a sweet taste.

Sounds pretty good, but let's face it: the Israelites had to endure much hardship living in the desert for forty years, including having a limited, albeit plentiful, menu from which to choose.

Panhandling under the bridge

I was driving a group of people into the city to serve dinner at one of the homeless shelters on a Friday night. As we exited the freeway and entered the city street system, we were stopped by a traffic light on

THOSE PEOPLE

a street adjacent to the freeway bridge, which was just above us and to the left. My vehicle was first in line at the stoplight, and as I pulled up I noticed a man holding a small sign made out of cardboard. I glanced at the digital thermometer in the rear view mirror of my vehicle that displayed the outside air temperature. It was -13 degrees Fahrenheit. That was without the wind chill.

I routinely stop for panhandlers. I try to connect with each one, learn his or her name, and exchange mine. I offer to shake hands. Rather than randomly hoping I have something to give, I am typically prepared with socks or a fast-food gift card. I prefer to give something I believe will be useful rather than cash.

Tangent alert!

I'm not totally opposed to giving cash to someone standing at an intersection and holding a sign that indicates he or she would like some assistance. I said not totally. This is a question that comes up regularly.

If you are asking the question, it might mean that this is a situation you encounter often enough that you sense the dilemma and aren't quite sure what is the "right" thing to do. You may have either read or heard of panhandlers who live in the suburbs and collect upwards of $100,000 per year by hustling drivers with a sad story of financial hardship and the need to support the family. Or you may be concerned about the legitimacy of the request and that the panhandler is simply going to take your cash and exchange it for drugs or alcohol. Not only do you not want to be duped, you have no desire to contribute to the harm of that person by feeding their habit or addiction.

If you've had these discussions either in your head or with others, stick with me and consider this approach.

With giving cash comes responsibility—not by the panhandlers but by you. If you have considered this quandary, then I contend that

More powerful than a locomotive (stamina)

you have a duty to take a position. Sure, you could take the position that you are going to turn your head and ignore these folks when you encounter them at a stoplight. But I don't see that as much of an option. If you are interested enough to read this book, then you need some other options. If you don't like the idea of giving out cash, what would you be willing to give that keeps you from feeling like you might be doing the wrong thing yet allows you to provide some help and encouragement?

Here's what I do—and feel free to come up with your own solutions. I always keep two things with me when I'm driving: clean, new socks and fast-food gift cards with enough funds on them to pay for one meal. The gift cards are $5.00, which can be a little spendy if you run into this often. The socks cost about $7.50 or $8.00 for a pack of ten cotton crew socks. One size fits most people. When I'm traveling out of town and may not be as prepared as I am when I'm home, I do give cash from time to time. And sometimes I don't have anything including cash. Even in those instances, I often stop, tell the person my name, tell them I have no cash or anything else to offer at the moment (only when this is the truth), explain that I'm sorry I have nothing to offer, and let them know I hope they are able to get what they need from the other passersby. It is amazing how often I give nothing other than my encouragement and that it is enough.

Since this is a common topic or question, I've included an appendix (page 149) outlining some principles, thoughts, and concrete ideas on interfacing with panhandlers.

Back to the bridge

I rolled down the window of my truck and introduced myself to the man holding the sign. He told me his name was "Chief," which I naturally assumed was not his real name, but in the short time we would have to visit, there was little chance of me learning more.

THOSE PEOPLE

I asked him where he was planning to stay for the night. That's a common question I like to ask. It gives me a little information about the person and his or her situation. The question is just personal enough to demonstrate my concern, but not so much that I'm getting into their business. Chief pointed to the west and explained he was staying under a bridge, one that brings a freeway from the west suburbs into the city. I must have seemed alarmed when I told him the current temperature (remember it was -13 degrees Fahrenheit) because he seemed to take on a calm almost nonchalant demeanor. I could be totally wrong about this, but he almost seemed to want to keep me from worrying.

"That's alright," Chief said. "I know what I'm doing. I've done this for a long time."

He wasn't fazed a bit. This was like every other day, just a little colder. I gave Chief some socks and gift cards, told him we'd pray for him, and that I'd try to find him later in the weekend. We did pray for Chief after serving our meal at the shelter. I wondered and worried the whole rest of the evening. When I slipped into my warm, soft, comfortable bed that night, I felt so unworthy of the comfort. Why me? Why do I enjoy this and others like Chief are struggling? A big question that doesn't have an easy answer.

I actually did find Chief a couple of days later. I trolled around the area about the same time and place, and on the second day I found him. I pulled into a nearby parking lot and walked back to have a proper conversation with him. Chief explained, again in a very casual way, that he didn't like the shelter system. He said he'd rather stay outside, and he had a bit of a camp put together to shield him and his friends from the wind and cold. They had some makeshift tents and tarps along with sleeping bags. For the cold, they build a fire, warm up, and then slip into their shelters and sleeping bags for the night. Frankly I don't care how he tried to explain it to me, it still sounds very cold, uncomfortable, and even dangerous. There's no way I'd suggest this is

More powerful than a locomotive (stamina)

a good life for Chief and his companions, but they have made it their choice from among their limited options. They are survivors.

In the summer of 2017, Chief was in his camp where he lived year-round. I don't know all the details surrounding what happened, but he was attacked and beaten to death by some guys known to him. I heard a couple accounts of the motive—jealously over a woman, offended about something, power struggle—however, in any case, the dispute came to a tragic ending.

When a person is poor, or mega-poor such as many of the homeless, there's not much done in the event of death. Sometimes the person's remains are buried in a publicly owned cemetery. There may be some attempt to notify next of kin. No obituary is posted because of the expense. I find that people living on the street sometimes just disappear. I always hope the best for them, as is sometimes the case, and I worry about the worst. We know people who are connected with a group that knew Chief, so word came quickly in this case, as to what happened.

The folks from Project 6:8,[3] along with Chief's friends and loved ones, organized a small ceremony for him. The local basilica agreed to allow the use of their lawn to stage the outdoor event. There were at least seventy-five people in attendance, maybe more. All were grieving. All were mourning. Many were hurt and angry at the perpetrators. Word was getting around about who this might be.

This series of events was a stark reminder to me that life on the street is hard, and even dangerous. And that providing aid, comfort, and friendship to those subjected to this lifestyle is serious business.

Dinner under the bridge

Project 6:8 is one of the ministries with which I'm involved. Since 2007 this small group of dedicated volunteers has faithfully served a warm, home-cooked meal under a bridge in Minneapolis—in rain, snow, or shine. Since they've been at it so long, there is a group of "alumni" that comes from time to time, even though they may not be in need of the support any longer, just to enjoy the fellowship.

There is a group of folks served by this ministry that stays out in the Minnesota elements year around. They have a small camp, where they keep their belongings, and cover up with tarps for shelter to supplement the use of a freeway bridge overpass. Small fires or a cook stove provide heat in the winter along with multiple layers of clothing. It seems impossible to me that anyone could survive a Minnesota winter totally outdoors with limited shelter. I have been reminded by some of the campers that their ancestors survived on less. (Many of our guests are of Native American heritage.) Good point, I guess, but still unbelievable to me.

We provide as much as we can based on their requests to help them be as comfortable as possible. They much prefer the out of doors than life inside one of the homeless shelters. Another good point. These are some tough and resilient people.

Going to summer camp

I never had the opportunity to go to summer camp. It just wasn't something we did or even really knew was an option for kids. But as I've gotten older and involved in my church and its men's group, I've stayed in camps many times. These are the same camps that young people frequent during the summer. Oftentimes a lake is on the property along with lots of outdoor activities like zip-lining, whiffle ball, shooting ranges, horseback riding, and the like. Knowing about these camps, if I could return to my childhood, I would totally beg to go.

The sleeping accommodations bear a vague resemblance to some of the homeless shelters I've been in. Or if you have served in the military, you might also be acquainted with barrack-style bunk rooms. There are lots of bunk beds, too many people to a room, and inadequate storage for belongings. You put a bunch of fully grown men into a room to sleep overnight, and you'll discover smells and sounds that barely seem human.

One of the worst parts is the "mattress." I use quotes because it's not really a mattress but more like a vinyl-covered mat. I understand that the construction of these must allow for easy and effective sanitation, but one sure gives up a lot in comfort for cleanliness.

With that said, I truly enjoy my time with other men when we're away at camp. When there, I have noted that the sleeping arrangement right down to the vinyl-covered mats is similar to how my homeless friends in shelters stay every evening. The difference is that when my enjoyable weekend is over, I go home to a warm, large, comfortable bed. Many nights when I've come home from visiting a homeless shelter and settle into bed, I think about the men that I just left less than an hour ago who are bedding down on one of the thin, plastic mats that I dislike so much. It's a humbling thought for me. And I appreciate and respect those men and women who tolerate that and still greet me with a smile at breakfast the next morning.

Doctor's orders: get some rest

My friend Jerry felt he was catching a cold. Within a few days, he felt it settle into his chest and was coughing up a lot of crud. After another day or two of this, he would cough and produce no crud. Jerry had pneumonia.

He went to the local hospital with an urgent care. This particular hospital in Minneapolis is the one that is designated for those who may not have the ability to pay for the services they need. It's actually a very good and reputable hospital. At times the hospital gets overrun by patients, and I'm sure it can be difficult to deliver great care all the time. When Jerry visited, he was quite sick. Fortunately he was prescribed and received a treatment of antibiotics. He was also prescribed rest. Lots of rest.

THOSE PEOPLE

I've had four bouts of pneumonia as an adult. For some reason, I am susceptible to this illness. Each time, I've seen a doctor, received doses of antibiotics, and gotten lots of rest. Rest, like sleep kind of rest. I've missed several days of work, and I've had someone to care for me.

When the homeless get sick, like Jerry with pneumonia, there is little rest. Usually lights out in a shelter is about 10:00 p.m. However, depending on the site, the staff may not enforce the "quiet down" policy so the people who choose to go to sleep are able to do so. There can be radios blaring and conversations happening well into the night. Granted it is hard to settle down 130–170 men or women who are all staying in the same room for the night. Again, depending on the shelter, discharge time can vary from 6:00-9:30 a.m. And even more challenging is that after getting a modest night's sleep, the homeless must get up, collect all their belongings, and carry them to some place outside and away from the shelter. So when a homeless person is sick or has the flu, I've seen it take a very long time, weeks or more, for his or her body to battle back against the illness and become well again.

It takes incredible physical stamina to be homeless and survive. I've seen this lifestyle prematurely diminish some of my friends, and I have little doubt, granted with no specific evidence, that long-term homelessness shortens and reduces the quality of a person's life. I have tremendous respect for my friends who endure this daily struggle, and I do my best to help in whatever way I can to create a small break or comfort as I'm able.

◦ ◦ ◦

CHALLENGE   Try fasting for one day, perhaps only drinking water. Each time you feel a hunger pang, turn your thoughts to the poor and homeless who often don't have the means or opportunity to eat or drink whenever they wish.

CHAPTER SIX

YOU'VE GOT TO HAVE . . .

(faith)

I've witnessed the faith lives on display with many of the folks I've encountered in the homeless community and through our work with people in our nonprofit social ministry, Threshold to New Life. The demonstration of having faith can be a funny thing. In one sense, it can seem that a person doesn't grasp the reality of the situation or maybe is experiencing a sense of denial about it. In other cases, there may be a quiet, confidence about the person, a sense of assurance that all will be well, whatever the outcome.

When researching the origin and meaning of the word *faith*, I found an interesting contrast in definitions.[1] First, faith is a "belief and trust in and loyalty to God." Second, it may also be a "firm belief in something for which there is no proof." Lastly, faith is "complete trust." No doubt, there is such a thing as faith without the need to believe in

God or another high power. The definition leaves plenty of room for that. But when one has faith in God, do you see how all three definitions actually fit together and in fact become a more complete definition? Faith is a belief and trust in God (first definition) when there is no or little proof (second definition) that the present circumstances will change or improve, which requires complete trust (third definition). I have witnessed those clients with a faith in God when there seems as though there is no other solution other than whatever he will provide. This complete definition is what I have witnessed in the lives of struggling people as I navigate through homeless shelters and spend time with those wrestling to meet the basic economic requirements to survive in this world.

Warning: history forthcoming

Faith is a controversial thing. So much so that it inflames those who claim they have no faith in God or any other higher being. The former professional wrestler and governor of Minnesota, Jessie Ventura, was famously quoted, "Organized religion is a sham and a crutch for weak-minded people who need strength in numbers."[2] I, too, have my concerns over "organized religion," but time and time again people such as Ventura develop personal attacks on whatever they choose not to believe. I am a fan of choice; and not having faith in God is a valid choice.

Jim Elliot is probably more famous for how he died than how he lived. Jim was a multitalented guy whose parents raised him and his siblings with a robust faith in God. Elliot felt God's calling to minister to an Ecuadorian indigenous tribe called the *Huaorani*. After some initial encounters with the tribe over several months, Jim and his ministerial companions were brutally murdered by the very people they intended to help. But the story didn't end there. Jim's new bride, Elisabeth, determined that the work God laid out for her husband must continue. Against conventional wisdom, Elisabeth reached out to the native people, the same tribe that killed her husband, and moved into the village along with their three-year-old daughter. It is widely thought that without the sacrifice made by Jim and the others earlier, that the Huaorani people may not have responded as they did to Elisabeth and the others that followed. The display of sacrificial love, a love grounded in faith and confidence in Christ, brought Elisabeth to the native people, and in turn they responded in love and respect for her.[3]

The apostle Paul provides excellent testimony of faith through trials in his letter to the Corinthians (see 2 Corinthians 11:16–33). Check out the suffering he endured because of his faith in Jesus:

> Five different times the Jewish leaders gave me thirty-nine lashes. Three times I was beaten with rods. Once I was stoned. Three times I was shipwrecked. Once I spent a whole night and a day adrift at sea. I have traveled on many long journeys. I have faced danger from rivers and from robbers. I have faced danger from my own people, the Jews, as well as from the Gentiles. I have faced danger in the cities, in the deserts, and on the seas. And I have faced danger from men who claim to be believers but are not. I have worked hard and long, enduring many sleepless nights. I have been hungry and thirsty and have often gone without food. I have shivered in the cold, without enough clothing to keep me warm. Then, besides all this, I have the daily burden of my concern for all the churches (2 Corinthians 11:24–28, NLT).

It would be difficult to argue that Paul is anything less than a "man's man," a rugged, tough, and bold campaigner of the cause for which he dedicated his later life. He was the first among many who followed in suffering for the sake of their great faith in Christ.

Many well-accomplished people have expressed their faith in Jesus throughout history, too many to name, but here are a few.

- C. S. Lewis: internationally renowned author, most famously for *The Chronicles of Narnia*.
- Galileo Galilei: noted astronomer, physicist, engineer, philosopher, and mathematician.

- Sir Isaac Newton: prominent scientist, discoverer of the force of gravity.

- Georges Cuvier: French naturalist and zoologist, sometimes referred to as the "father of paleontology."

- George Washington Carver: American scientist, botanist, educator, and inventor.

Actually, between the years 1901 and 2000, nearly two-thirds of Nobel Prize Laureates have identified Christianity as their religious preference.[4]

Is a faith in Jesus a crutch for weak-minded people? Well, you decide.

A peek inside

I like to think of prayer as a window to one's faith. We peek through the window, obscured more or less by the glass, and can see inside the dwelling. When I hear someone pray, it may not be a perfectly clear perspective on the person's faith, which is possibly obscured by what might be going on in the moment, the burdens and worries held by the individual, or simply the fear of loss of preservation of his or her life before things went sideways. But in any event, it is a glimpse into the faith of the person praying.

Larry is a thick fellow, with a massive, grey beard and hair to match. He has deep, blue, piercing eyes, and I wonder when he cleans up if he's quite a handsome guy. I'm not sure of his age, but I was told by another that he's in his mid- to late-fifties. Years on the street and a chronic addiction to alcohol have waged war on Larry's health and appearance.

There is one particular homeless shelter that he frequents, so when I find him, it's usually there. This shelter has an area designated for those who don't pass the Breathalyzer test. Failure of the test places one

You've got to have . . . (faith)

on the floor on a mat, as opposed to sleeping the night on a bunk bed. People sleeping on floor mats were under the influence when they arrived. The area becomes a kind of quarantine or purgatory for drunks, a further diminished subset of the homeless population in the shelter. When I'm looking for Larry, I search among the mats on the floor.

A couple of years ago one of the guys who serves in our breakfast ministry brought Larry along to our annual men's retreat sponsored by the church we attend together. Not only does this retreat have lots of activities like golf, paintball, zip-lining, and floor hockey, but there are presentations that are both inspiring and thought provoking. At this particular retreat, there was an exercise in which we were to pair off with one or two other guys, lay out our personal concerns that weighed heavy on our hearts, and then end with prayer for each other. Larry and one other guy formed my breakout group. I had known Larry for a while now, but honestly, I had never had a conversation with him that revealed anything about his faith or beliefs. I'm embarrassed now to think that was the case. I'm not sure why it hadn't happened earlier.

After Larry and the other guy spoke of their concerns and requests for prayer, we ended with my concern for my son, still in high school, who was in a period of sudden rebellion that we just didn't understand the source of or how to help him through it. Our family wanted desperately to connect with him, and by the time of the retreat, we were still very much in the dark about what to do. To me, there just seemed to be no end in sight and no clear solution. After I shared my concern, we went to prayer.

After the other guy prayed, it was Larry's turn. I regret that I don't know exactly what he said, but I distinctly remember the feeling when he finished. It was such a heartfelt prayer. A confident prayer. A loving prayer. A prayer prayed by someone with a great amount of empathy, concern, and love for me, my son, and my family. By the end, all three of us were weeping and hugging. I'll never forget it. Because of and through that prayer experience, Larry and I forged a bond that makes us like brothers. At the retreat we had been given bracelets, actually a thick, colored rubber band, to identify our groups. Larry and I had different colors and were in different groups for all the rest of the activities, other than the prayer time. Now a few years later, he still wears his bracelet, as do I. When we see each other, we check each other out to see that the bracelet is still intact. I lost mine a year ago so I replaced it, since I had become used to wearing one the past couple of years. And I want to honor my friend Larry by continuing to wear a bracelet.

Due to Larry's faith and bold prayer, I received a gift of God's grace, something I didn't expect or request. And my son? He's great! Graduated from high school and on to college. He even asked me to have dinner with him once a month so we can stay connected to each other. How's that for a miracle?

Just delivering a couch

Threshold to New Life works to eliminate gaps in people's lives. We focus primarily on housing and specifically on helping people, homeless in their recent past, keep the housing they already have. There is a huge amount of churn in the homeless community that I see firsthand. People obtain housing, either a modest apartment or a room at a multi-tenant housing location, and they end up returning to the shelter within months to a couple of years later. Why? A multitude of reasons. First is the lack of affordable housing, and in metropolitan areas like Minneapolis-St. Paul, it's even more challenging. Many can't find suitable work, meaning a job that will pay enough to maintain an apartment and the usual living expenses we all have. Although the changes in the healthcare system are intended to help those without healthcare, it also seems to have created some unintended negative consequences, one of which is that many employers only hire people for twenty-nine hours or less per week to avoid paying for healthcare. It's tough to make a living at a modestly paying job, especially when it's not quite full time either. There are certainly other challenges, but these are primary.[5]

From time to time, we do provide things at Threshold to New Life other than rent assistance. Our hope is to keep our overhead costs low, so we don't actually have a physical location. That can be hampering at times, especially when we have someone who would like to donate something really useful and we don't have a place to store it. I should note, however, we break this rule from time to time. We actually have one bedroom and a large portion of our garage dedicated to storing items. Our ideal situation is when we have a need to fill, we put the word out to our network of followers, and someone emerges with a way to fill the need.

Mary needed a couch and chair for her new apartment. We alerted our friends and followers to the need, and wouldn't you know, someone we remotely knew was in the process of downsizing and wanted to donate a couch and chair. We assembled a couple of folks to help with the move, got a truck, and picked up the furniture. We arrived at Mary's shortly thereafter and moved it in and placed it as she wished. Our work was done except for one last thing.

Typically, as we finish helping a client with a need, we explain who we are and why we do what we do. We tell them that our faith motivates us to give of our time and treasure and that the early church provided for those who had needs, so we're stepping into people's lives to help in a similar way. We never push our beliefs or attempt to convert anyone. We just say who we are and why we do what we do. We offer prayer too. I like to ask the question: "If you could bring anything before God today, anything at all, what would you like to ask of him?" The responses to that question are remarkable. And Mary was no exception.

She cried. My wife, Carla, rubbed her shoulder and Mary explained her prayer request. She asked us to pray for God to be with her grandchildren. She had some concerns about their well-being and asked that we pray for them. Then she said, "I have a chemo appointment today. I have a ride lined up already. I'm being treated for breast cancer. It's stage four. I would like to pray for healing but mostly for God's will to be done, whatever that is." As she said this, the rest of us began to get emotional. We went to prayer.

It's a powerful and awesome thing to physically connect with other people either by holding hands or with arms around shoulders while bringing our worries, cares, and concerns before the God of the entire universe. It was a moving moment for each person there as well as for Mary. It's not uncommon to get requests for prayer for others when we offer to pray. I always think that is amazing in itself. When you're struggling to make it and the first thought on your mind is to pray for others? Again, my experience is that the poor and struggling often think of others first.

And for Mary, concern for her grandchildren was paramount on her mind. Even before prayer for her personal health or healing from cancer, she wanted God to intervene in her grandchildren's lives.

Saying grace

Serving breakfast at a homeless shelter is really a hoot. We arrive an hour beforehand, cook and prep, and then we serve for an hour and clean up for half an hour. As our guests arrive just before our serving time of 5:30 a.m., they line up outside until the shelter staff permits them in. Those staying in the shelter line up in the lobby. When 5:30 a.m. arrives, our guests come into the cafeteria and line up in front of our two stainless steel serving tables. Usually one person on our team will announce, "Line up and we'll bless the food and get started!"

Whenever possible, we attempt to identify someone among our guests to say the blessing over the meal. We don't instruct people to bow their heads or anything, we just offer up the prayer and move

You've got to have ... (faith)

immediately into serving breakfast. Sometimes we can't get a volunteer to step up, but surprisingly, we often do. I know lots of people in my faith community who don't or won't pray in public, even in a small group. I guess there's some pressure about sounding dumb or getting tongue-tied. Within the homeless ranks, we find lots of folks who are willing to pray out loud in a group setting. Why is that? Your guess is as good as mine.

On this particular Sunday, we had a full house. It was February, late in the month, which means the shelter was full to capacity. Those receiving any sort of a payment, whether general assistance or a disability payment, often leave the shelter system at the beginning of the month, perhaps to stay at a hotel, just to get a little relief. When the money runs out, they return to the shelter. It's a monthly cycle. When its cold outside, as it typically is during February in Minnesota, the weather also leads people to the shelters, for the obvious reason. So, like I said, we were full.

Shauna is a small, middle-age, African American woman with a huge, loud voice. I've often wondered if she could carry a tune, because if she could sing, she'd make a great blues lead singer. She has that raspy, deep voice, much larger than her appearance. Once in a while Shauna can get a little riled up, and when she does, everyone knows it. I made a general request to the group to ask if anyone would offer to bless the meal before we started. Sometimes there's a particular person I know who is willing so I simply ask him or her. There are certain people whose prayers I just enjoy hearing, and there are several at this particular shelter that fall into that category. Shauna stepped forward and said she'd do it. I didn't even get time to tell her to go ahead, and she shouted out, "Hey, y'all, I'm going to pray so these people can serve us breakfast! So bow your heads!" How's that for direction?

Then Shauna let out this loud and proud prayer. Remember I said that prayer can be a window into the faith of a person? I learned some things about Shauna that morning that I didn't know. I didn't know she would be bold enough to pray out loud in front of a large group of people. I also didn't know the depth of her faith and the heart she has. It became clear to me that she has studied God's word and has prayed often before. She's heard many other people pray before, too, so I'm sure she's learned a thing or two about public prayer by listening to others, which by the way, I have too. It was a great moment to experience, and I can only imagine God smiled when he heard that prayer by Shauna.

Pray to start, pray to end

We pray as we open our breakfast, and we also pray as we end. After about a half hour of clean up, our volunteer crew is ready to take off. We wrap up every day about 7:00 a.m. The most stalwart volunteer is Jerry (more about him in another chapter). Here, I only want to reveal his heart for prayer and what it means to our volunteers.

As we wrap up our daily breakfast every morning, Jerry is the single, consistent link among all the teams. He is the only person who serves daily and has met all the regularly committed volunteers. We have a small building, on loan to our group from the Salvation Army, in which we store and stage our supplies. All the food preparation is done in the commercial kitchen in the shelter across the street. But each day begins and ends in our little building on Currie Avenue.

Once we've washed our cooking pots and utensils in the commercial kitchen, we bring our gear back across the street to our building. We have several garden wagon-style carts to haul what we need back and forth. It often takes multiple trips before we're ready to cook and serve, and several trips back to our building once we're finished. Our team works together after our serving is complete to stage the carts for the next day's crew. When they arrive at 4:30 a.m. the following day, we aim to have everything ready so they can simply pull the wagons across the street and get started with the food preparation.

You've got to have ... (faith)

When we're wrapped up with staging, we gather in the main room of our building to debrief on the day. We ask the group if anyone brought a prayer request to them or if any of us have something we want to bring to God in prayer that occurred to us that day while serving. We then move into prayer requests for our team. Jerry, being the only link among the teams, updates each day's team on the goings-on with other days' team members. If there is a prayer request from one team, Jerry is the one who delivers this to the other teams. We've had folks with cancer and other serious health issues, and Jerry has brought this up to each team so that we pray seven days a week for the needs of our teammates.

Then Jerry leads us in prayer. His gentle, quiet spirit and the pureness of his heart and intentions are on full display. Jerry is a guy who seems to love everyone and has empathy for all who have needs. He prays out loud while the rest of our team members listen; he petitions God for his involvement in what we do, to provide relief to those we serve and to meet the needs of those on our team. It's a beautiful thing to witness and an honor to be part of a daily team and to be a participant while Jerry leads us in prayer.

Down in the dumps

It's actually stunning that it doesn't happen more often—running into someone in a homeless shelter who's bummed out. One would think this is commonplace, and sure, I do encounter people who are down or discouraged. But on the whole, a vast majority of folks I deal with on a regular basis smile easily and are interested to have a conversation. My friend Vinny is generally one of those who I would consider a positive person and even lighthearted. Not on this occasion.

Vinny and I had spent several evenings before this particular one, sharing our struggles, our faith, and our hope for the future. Less than a year earlier, he had had his own apartment and now found himself back in a homeless shelter. This wasn't his first time homeless, but he felt that the last time he was homeless that he didn't ever want to return. But here he was again. And for whatever reason, on this evening he was pretty down.

His big question was, "Does God still love me and does he care about my needs? Can he really have an effect on what's going on in my life?" Actually this is a really big question that most of us have wrestled with in times of struggle. Navigating the ups and downs (mainly the downs) in this world can feel like riding a rollercoaster without a safety bar in front to hold. On this evening, Vinny's rollercoaster was picking up speed, going downhill fast, and he didn't seem to have anything holding him in his seat.

I'm not the type of person who uses an approach with hurting people where I try to find a relevant Bible passage, quote it to the individual, and then expect that ... boom ... there's your answer. Isn't that grand! Now the person knows what to do and what God will be doing, so he or she can start feeling better. I think doing that is a real disservice to hurting people. And for people who are really struggling in their faith, it can have the effect of pushing them away from God altogether. When God and his Word are presented like this, it can seem distant and disingenuous. I know that God isn't either of those things. I try to show up in hurting people's lives as the Spirit leads me. One of the names Jesus gave for the Holy Spirit is "Comforter."[6] So I try to show up as a comforter in these situations. After I listened to Vinny's concerns, let him vent his frustrations, and share his hurts and worries, there was a passage in Scripture that occurred to me. Since Vinny and I had enjoyed a number of times in which we shared our thoughts on Bible passages, I carefully suggested I thought there was a passage in Scripture that might speak to his situation.

You may already know the story of Job, but let me set the stage so I can weave it into my story about Vinny.

You've got to have . . . (faith)

Job's story

Job was a really, really good guy. He was rich, had a big family, and a successful business, and along with that he didn't fall into the trappings or temptations of success. Like I said, he was just a great person. Through a strange, cosmic arrangement, God allowed Satan to tempt Job because God was so confident in Job's faith. So Job lost nearly everything—money, home, business, children, and even his health—in a tragic and swift series of events. In those times (maybe now, too?) people associated good coming to people because they were good and did good things. And the converse as well: bad things came to those who were bad and did bad. When this tragedy suddenly fell into Job's life, his friends and close associates took notice, confronted Job, and urged him to admit what he'd done wrong, as it was the only course of restoration. The problem was that Job didn't do anything to bring the calamity onto himself or his family, so he didn't have anything to admit. And he certainly didn't have any idea why all the bad things were happening to him. After a dialogue in which Job outlined every possible wrong one could imagine and yet didn't admit to any wrongdoing, he heard God's powerful reply.

God seemed to have heard enough of Job's challenges and decided to put Job in his place by asking him a series of rhetorical, pointed questions through which God's strength and sovereignty were revealed. Here's a taste of the dialogue:

> "Where were you when I laid the foundation of the earth?
> Tell me, if you have understanding.
> Who determined its measurements—surely you know!
> Or who stretched the line upon it?
> On what were its bases sunk,
> or who laid its cornerstone,
> when the morning stars sang together
> and all the sons of God shouted for joy?
>
> "Or who shut in the sea with doors
> when it burst out from the womb,

THOSE PEOPLE

> when I made clouds its garment
> and thick darkness its swaddling band,
> and prescribed limits for it
> and set bars and doors,
> and said, 'Thus far shall you come, and no farther,
> and here shall your proud waves be stayed'?
>
> "Have you commanded the morning since your days began,
> and caused the dawn to know its place,
> that it might take hold of the skirts of the earth,
> and the wicked be shaken out of it?
> It is changed like clay under the seal,
> and its features stand out like a garment.
> From the wicked their light is withheld,
> and their uplifted arm is broken.
>
> "Have you entered into the springs of the sea,
> or walked in the recesses of the deep?
> Have the gates of death been revealed to you,
> or have you seen the gates of deep darkness?
> Have you comprehended the expanse of the earth?
> Declare, if you know all this.
>
> "Where is the way to the dwelling of light,
> and where is the place of darkness,
> that you may take it to its territory
> and that you may discern the paths to its home?
> You know, for you were born then,
> and the number of your days is great!
>
> "Have you entered the storehouses of the snow,
> or have you seen the storehouses of the hail,
> which I have reserved for the time of trouble,
> for the day of battle and war?
> What is the way to the place where the light is distributed,
> or where the east wind is scattered upon the earth? (Job 38:4–24, ESV).

You've got to have . . . (faith)

These verses are about half of one of the two chapters I read aloud to Vinny and to a small group of others who gathered and listened as I read God's words to Job. God's words emphasize his strength and stability that he exercises in all sorts of situations; that he is so much larger than us; and that it's absolutely ridiculous for us to think anything other than that. When I finished reading, we all marveled at the passage and how God loves us so much that he wants to remind us he's in control.

At the end of our impromptu Bible study, a small crowd had gathered around Vinny's bunk. I asked a question that I love to ask, because I've heard the answer a number of times and it's always heartening and amusing to me to hear it: "If Jesus were to return tonight, where do you think he'd go first? Would he go to the basilica, over to First Baptist Church, or would he come to this homeless shelter?" The men smiled and they all nodded in agreement, "He'd come to this shelter first!" offered one fellow. The others just smiled. They just might be right.

And by the way, Vinny was encouraged that night. We embraced as I was leaving, and he thanked me for the good word delivered. A couple of months later, Vinny got a new place and moved out of the shelter.

○   ○   ○

CHALLENGE   Next time someone is sharing with you his or her concerns, be it a coworker, one of your children, a friend, or whoever, be patient, listen, and resist offering advice. After you've listened, tell them, "Wow, that sounds really tough. I'm so sorry you're going through that." I'm still surprised that seems to be enough in many cases; just listening and being concerned is what people desire, and not necessarily advice.

CHAPTER SEVEN

THE HEART OF THE MATTER

(serving)

Serving others can be considered a critical element in a healthy, well-adjusted person's life. A blog by the Huffington Post in 2015 listed seven reasons why volunteering leads to a better life for the volunteer. Among the benefits of volunteering noted are less stress, more happiness, a longer life, better physical and physiological health, and even advancement in one's career.[1] A person does not need to come from a background in faith or a belief in God or other higher power to come to the conclusion that it's a good thing to serve. Even if the one being served is ultimately the server.

People who profess to follow Jesus and his teachings are urged to have a different perspective on serving. In Jesus, we see the greatest example of a servant. He told his followers at that time that "the Son of Man came not to be served but to serve, and to give his life as a ransom for many" (Matthew 20:28, ESV). Not only did he say this, but he followed this up with action.

Barefoot party

Here's the scene. Jesus is hosting a dinner party, the last one he will have on earth, and he knows it. He secured a room above someone's home to hold the gathering with his closest disciples—the top twelve people in his following. He's lived, worked, slept, eaten, taught, and traveled with these guys for the past three years. Now it's time for his farewell. Jesus knows what the next day's events will bring. In spite of this knowledge, he humbles himself in this last gathering with his friends to serve them. How?

Tradition of the time would call for a washing of one's feet prior to entering a home as a guest. Think of it as walking into a stranger's home where you have been invited. All you see ahead of you is light-colored carpet, so you kick your shoes off in the entryway on the linoleum-clad floor. Your shoes probably aren't covered with dirt and animal feces (unless you're a farmer, sorry, that's cool) as would be the feet of Jesus' guests. Without paved roads and with animals and people sharing the same routes, people's feet could get pretty nasty. So when one would go inside a residence, each person would wash his or her feet before entering. If the host had the wealth to maintain a household staff, it would be the job of one of the servants to wash the feet of each guest. When there was more than one household staff, the job would fall to the lowest servant. It was the least desirable job of all—one rung below the servant that carried out the contents of the indoor toilet to be dumped. Jesus took on the lowest position of all. He humbled himself to serve those who dropped everything and walked away from their lives three years earlier to follow him. He washed their feet (see John 13:1-17).

The heart of the matter (serving)

The least of these

This wasn't the only time Jesus weighed in on serving. He also provided a bit of a warning.

In the middle chapters of the Gospel of Matthew, Jesus addresses the Jewish establishment, the scribes, the Sadducees, and the Pharisees to whom he provided several teachings and warnings. The Jewish leaders tried to trip him up on questions, such as: Should people pay all their taxes to the government as demanded? Of all the commandments God provided, which is the greatest? Jesus navigated through these questions with responses that are clever, wise, and true. He then revealed what it would be like when he returns, and how he'll separate the sheep from the goats. Metaphorically this could mean the true followers of Jesus who pattern their lives after his as they follow him, and the pretenders who might do good things, but believe in themselves that they are right enough to enter his kingdom. We might conclude this because when Jesus was later alone with his followers, he stated, "For I was hungry and you gave me food, I was thirsty and you gave me drink, I was a stranger and you welcomed me, I was naked and you clothed me, I was sick and you visited me, I was in prison and you came to me" (Matthew 25:35–36, ESV). Seems such an odd thing to say. Who among them had seen their Lord in any of these situations? Jesus answered his own question: "Truly, I say to you, as you did it to one of the least of these my brothers, you did it to me" (Matthew 25:40, ESV).

That's a bombshell unleashed. Jesus was taking the position that as we are serving others who have needs (like the ones he mentioned) it is the same as serving Jesus directly. That sure puts a lot of weight and emphasis on serving as we follow Jesus.

Slave vs. servant

There are two different words in the Greek language, the language in which the original books of the New Testament were written, to describe a person who serves. The first is *diokonas*, which roughly means someone who executes the commands of another.[2] There is no implication of mastery over the servant. It simply means this person serves because he or she is expected to serve. An example would be a modern-day waiter.

But that's not the term adopted by the early followers of Jesus. In the Bible that term is *doulos*, which is to be taken in a very different context. *Doulos* literally means a slave, a person without any ownership rights of his or her own.[3] A doulos is the property of another person. More pointedly, a doulos is a bond servant of his or her master. There is a price to pay to be released from this slavery. The early followers of Jesus used this term to describe themselves and their relationship with Jesus after his resurrection. Even though their debt was paid through Jesus' blood shed on the cross, they remained in his service. Why would that be?

Simple. They loved Jesus. They were not obligated to serve him because the debt was paid. They served him out of love. Serving Jesus out of obligation doesn't cut it. We could never do enough to balance the ledger of our lives: all the things we've done wrong, the people we've hurt, the things we should have done, and so on. Serving Jesus out of love is allowing him to exercise Lordship in our lives, not just that we're following the rules so we're "good people."

The truth is, not all serving opportunities are happy, joyous, and carefree. Serving people can be messy work. It can be hard, exhausting, and discouraging at times. Sure, we hope to see in the folks we serve something that resembles results, even if it's a simple "thank you." But if we focus on Jesus' words—serving others in need is equal to or the same as serving Jesus directly—we can get less tangled up in the here and now and be assured that we're serving Jesus himself. And he'll take care of the "results" of our effort.

The heart of the matter (serving)

Homeless serving homeless

How is it that the homeless serve? And why?

At our events, usually centered around food, it's common to have people who are part of the clientele be willing to step in to provide assistance. My thought is that we are hardwired to be helpful, and serving others is a way to do that. Most people feel better about themselves when they have an opportunity to contribute by helping to serve. It improves one's outlook on things, and even one's self-perception can improve. The world doesn't seem like such a grim place when we're helpful.

I have also experienced several homeless and struggling folks step up to help because of their *doulos* relationship to Jesus. It can be awkward for someone living in a shelter to step forward to provide assistance to peers coming in. It can even get a little petty. I've heard people called names and insulted simply for coming from the ranks of the shelter to pitch in when our volunteer staff may be short-handed. For those whose service is to the one who paid the debt they couldn't, well, it makes it more tolerable.

Chance encounter

We've had several folks jump in to help us set up for our daily breakfast. One of the fellow's name was Chance. Yeah, I know, there are lots of people living on the street who have nicknames or "handles," but really, the guy showed me his state ID card and his middle name is actually the name he is called: Chance.

He was only around for a couple of weeks, but he was very helpful at a time the daily teams really needed him. He is a big and gregarious guy with a personality fitting his name. One morning I was coming into the shelter about 4:30 a.m., and I hadn't yet seen any of my teammates. So I was dragging all the gear to cook and serve more than one hundred people across the street on my own. "Can I help?" Chance asked. Naturally I accepted. Unless we're totally flush with volunteers, if any one of the residents demonstrating a reasonable attitude offers to help, we typically find something for him or her to do.

As I mentioned, Chance was only around for a few weeks then he disappeared. I only saw him one other time, a couple of months later. He was with his girlfriend sitting across the street from the same homeless shelter one evening while the lineup to go in was starting. I recognized him immediately, and I certainly remembered his name. I greeted him and his friend and asked if I could have a seat. He was pretty discouraged about some things going on in his life. I listened for a long time and told him I was very sorry about all of that. Chance was trying to connect some of the current events in his life to Scripture he had read previously and was having a hard time putting things together. He asked if I was a pastor. I told him no, but I offered to tell him what I knew from the Bible that might relate to his situation. We talked more and I shared with him some things I knew from Scripture that I thought applied to him. He and his friend cried a bit and I offered to pray. So across from the shelter during the lineup, we held hands and prayed. He wanted to.

I haven't seen Chance since. It's always bittersweet to have someone come into your life from a shelter then suddenly disappear. I always hope it's for the best and good reason. I hope to see him again, but in a better circumstance.

High energy

Casey has been helping us cook and serve for the past six months. Wow, does that guy have a motor . . . and it always seems to be running.

I don't know too much of Casey's backstory except that he's in his mid-thirties and is receiving disability payments. He seems a bit

The heart of the matter (serving)

quirky at times; maybe excitable is a better description. He appears to be physically fit and he moves well—I mean he moves fast! So whatever his disability is, it doesn't appear to be physical. In most cases, I don't ask for the sake of embarrassing the person. But he chose to tell me that he is on disability.

Casey stayed at the shelter for a while, which is how he came to know about our breakfast. When he got his own place, he moved to Saint Paul, just across the Mississippi River and adjacent to Minneapolis. For Casey to serve with us, he must get up around 3:30 a.m. to catch a bus to bring him to the shelter. When I arrive most mornings, he's sitting outside, smoking a cigarette, waiting for me to open up our storage building.

Casey shared with me one day that one of the volunteers on another day's crew had offended him. When I asked how, he said that he had asked if he could get a dollar or two for bus fare. Our volunteers are discouraged from carrying cash and specifically asked not to give out money. We're there to serve a meal and have fellowship with our patrons. If we start giving out cash, well, it never ends. Then the whole event is about giving out money, who's giving out money, how much money one person gets, and so on. We just don't give out cash—that's how we've coached our team. So when Casey asked for cash, he was given a flat "no." That's why he was upset. He told me if he was going to help he didn't expect to pay out of his pocket for transportation. Yup, I get it. In this case, I think he was right.

I purchase and carry bus tokens with me when I'm downtown visiting a shelter or serving. A bus token is good for one ride with no transfers and until recently has cost $1.75; now each token is $2.50. Our social ministry purchases these by the hundreds, and I always keep some with me. There are several organizations that hand out bus tokens to folks in need downtown. There's a street value to the tokens, too. I have to admit I don't know exactly what one will get in exchange for a token, but I know tokens can be exchanged for cash, cigarettes, drugs, or alcohol. So giving a token to someone needing a ride is one thing. To give one to someone hustling you for tokens is another. It's not always easy to tell the difference as much as I try.

I explained to Casey the guidelines we give to our volunteers and why we enforce them. Then I told him I generally have bus tokens with me, and I would be glad to give him a few when he serves with me. When we have a repeating volunteer from among the ranks we're serving, I like to encourage them by helping to meet one of his or her needs, something special that I may not give out to everyone. It might be a jacket, backpack, or toiletries kit. I usually carry those items with me, but I don't have a hundred or more to share with the masses. I let them pick out whatever they say they need.

Casey understood and I gave him a couple of tokens.

A couple of months later I was told by another shelter resident that Casey was a junkie, a habitual drug user, and that he trades in the tokens I give him for drugs. Ugh. I hate these dilemmas. Too often I'm put in a position of feeling the need to judge what is right and actually help people or what is hurtful and enabling. That's one of the reasons I don't give out cash frequently. Instead I try to give a useful item such as a bus token or a gift card good for a meal. I realize the last two items can be exchanged for drugs or alcohol, but I guess I feel I'm one step removed from that and the individual then has to choose the right thing. I honestly can't even say I'm right about all this. It's just what I do currently.

I agonized about this recently learned information during the morning breakfast. I prayed silently and asked God to show me what he would have me do—give tokens and have Casey convert these to drugs or booze or not give the tokens and run the risk of losing him as a volunteer and offending him as well. I like to say that I often try to "err on the side of grace," meaning if I'm not sure what to do, I do what I believe is helpful rather than stand in judgment about the person and not deliver to them what I have to offer. So at the end of the morning shift, I offered Casey a couple tokens. "Thanks, I'm good," he said to me.

Really?

He reams me out a couple of months earlier when he was put off by one of our volunteers for not helping him with transportation costs ... I offered to help ... then I'm encouraged to think he's a hustler ... so faced with the moral decision of whether or not to offer him bus tokens again ... and finally, at the end of all this, he says he's "good," meaning he doesn't need tokens today. Man, confusing. But the exchange did offer me a crisp, moment of clarity. If Casey were trading tokens for illicit items, wouldn't he take all he could get, even if he didn't need them for bus fare? Why would he turn them down?

In the end I really don't know. And I don't know for sure what Casey does with the bus tokens. I do believe it's a good sign that he doesn't take them every time I offer. So, perhaps I'm doing the right thing? I don't know for sure, but it's the best I can come up with. Serving people can be a messy and imprecise business.

Serving with heart (trouble)

Cecil began to show up a few years ago to help serve when we were short staffed. It's a welcome offer when we have too few hands to help and someone volunteers. I suppose Cecil was a regular for more than a year, maybe two years. He found us through his time in a shelter, and then he moved into a neighboring, subsidized building, so he lived just around the corner from our breakfast. Our breakfast is a community breakfast, so even though we serve out of one homeless shelter, we allow anyone to come and join us. We do get people from Cecil's building enjoying our breakfast each day. Even though we serve very early in the morning, the price is always right.

THOSE PEOPLE

Cecil was a tall, African American guy with a huge smile. He wore glasses and had almost a gangly look to him. Cecil spoke superfast, almost as if he was spitting the words out in chunks. You know when someone is winded and trying to talk? The person tends to try to jam as many words in the breath he or she just took, then pause to breathe again, and then send out another burst of words. That's Cecil's regular, everyday diction.

He was about the same age as me at the time, guessing early fifties, and he struggled with heart issues. He told me the doctors were concerned about his sleep and asked him to do a sleep study. He was also on several medications, for blood pressure and the like. Looking at him, I wouldn't put him in a physically unhealthy category, but for some reason he had all these ailments.

Cecil shared with me that he struggled with drug addiction. He had been working to stay clean, but I honestly don't know how successful he was. I heard rumors that he was still using. Remember the rumor about Casey? Well, I take it as information but not necessarily reliable. I can say that I never once experienced Cecil under the influence of anything. That's how I knew him.

When a person is poor, the healthcare provided isn't the same quality as people who have money. It's just a fact of the system. Our government has tried to intervene in this, but even in countries that have some version of "socialized medicine," wealthy people pay to jump ahead in the system or pay to receive their healthcare in another country. In Minneapolis the brunt of the healthcare for the poor is fulfilled at Hennepin County Medical Center (HCMC). The hospital is actually well known and respected in the medical community. But because it is a publicly funded hospital in an urban area, it must shoulder the healthcare needs of those who can least afford it.

A few times I've been at HCMC with people waiting to be seen by a care provider. The key word in the last sentence is *waiting*. There's

The heart of the matter (serving)

a lot of waiting going on. Imagine a hospital serving a population of several hundred thousand people, and of those, several thousand don't have health insurance or the means to pay for their care—it's a challenge to provide good quality and timely care. I think the staff at HCMC really does their best on the whole, but I also believe the quality of care for the "haves" is better than the "have nots." Cecil was obviously in the latter category.

To help Cecil with his sleep, for at least a week he wore the sleep monitor that he was issued. It recorded his movements and vitals while he slept, if he slept. He also did a sleep study and received a CPAP machine to treat what was diagnosed as sleep apnea. Cecil had a hard time adapting to the use of the machine. He was always very nervous about the quality of the care he received and questioned a number of the decisions the care providers urged him into. A couple of times he asked my advice. Man, I really didn't want to be put on the spot to offer advice to accept this treatment or pass on this test when I'm not a medical doctor and I'm not the one even being treated. I guess I dodged his questions by suggesting that if it *were* me, here's what I would do. And I would encourage him to question his doctors more.

You may have noticed that I describe Cecil in the past tense. It's not because he's no longer one of our regular volunteers. It's because he is no longer. Cecil died in his apartment of a heart attack in the early morning hours on a warm August summer day. His cousin Vinny told me about it that evening when I was visiting another shelter. Vinny and I were friends, and he was Cecil's uncle. He was the one who encouraged Cecil to come to Minneapolis, and Vinny kind of looked after him while he was here. It was a very somber night to say the least.

I really loved Cecil. His giant smile and fast-talking made him seem to me like a larger than life super happy guy. Often, he was that guy. He was someone we often counted on to fill a space at our servers' table. He was usually the cold cereal server. When he'd offer the three or four kinds of cereal to the next guest in line, I rarely could understand what he was saying, although most others seemed to. Would he still be alive if he had had the means or insurance to get more attention to his health issues? That's a question that will drive one crazy. I just know he was a really sweet guy. I miss him.

Seating arranger

I'm not sure exactly when Norm began to help, but it must have been when we moved the serving of our daily breakfast from the street to inside the shelter cafeteria. For the first eight years we had served breakfast out on the street in front of the shelter. We set up portable tables to serve from, and our patrons would stand and hold their meal in their hands while they ate, kind of a balancing act. Remember, this is Minnesota so we didn't hold our breakfast outside year around. Whenever the temperature was 50 degrees Fahrenheit or above, and it wasn't too windy or raining, we'd serve outside. This was roughly from about mid-April to sometime into October. For the other months, we served inside an overly crowded lobby. Again, we set up our folding serving tables, and folks would collect their breakfast and stand while they ate.

New leadership came to the shelter and with that a new partnership with our ministry. It took a little time, but eventually the new captain warmed to what we do and invited us to move our serving inside their cafeteria. I suspect another motivation was to help keep the streets clean. With one hundred people or more eating a daily meal on a public street using disposable bowls, spoons, and cups, well, many of those items ended up on the street and sidewalk. Our volunteers would do their best to pick up after people, but many folks need to run off to their jobs so hanging around picking up trash isn't on the agenda. Serving the meal inside means the street and sidewalk stay clean.

The heart of the matter (serving)

The logistics to serve inside changed our operation. Now we need to clean up the cafeteria before the staff serves their meal to the residents. The building is of mixed use. There are programs operating within the building that allow participates to reside there. There's also what is called "pay for stay" on the second floor, a place to live that isn't intended to be permanent, but one may live there until a place opens up or one qualifies for some other program. The first floor is the men's shelter and part of the third floor is a women's shelter. These shelter residents are not eligible for meals, only for the communal sleeping arrangements. Program and transitional housing people are the only ones that eat. That makes our meal even more important. Other shelters do provide meals—morning, evening, or both. This one happens to provide neither.

Norm began to help one day. The chairs in the cafeteria were all stacked up so that staff could mop the floor after the evening meal. Sometimes we only have two volunteers, and it can get a little hectic to get everything ready, so setting up chairs doesn't fit into the program. I thanked him and asked his name. When I came back the next time, Norm was doing it again: setting up chairs at 4:45 a.m. in the morning. He stays at the shelter and has no reason to be up that early to help us. Naturally, I thanked him. I asked some of our folks on other teams and yup, Norm was showing up other days to set up chairs too. Even when he had a cast—I can't remember for sure but I think it was a tendon issue in his ankle—he would hobble in with his cane and slowly set up chairs.

One day not long after we first met, Norm told me he had written something he wanted to share with me. Of course I agreed. He pulled out pages of a handwritten story he had written. I think it was an actual account of something in his life that was dated nearly twenty years earlier. He handed the pages to me and asked me to take them home, read them, and tell him what I thought. I resisted at first. This seemed like very precious cargo for him to share with me, since he barely knew me. I brought the pages home and read them. I have to admit I don't recall anymore exactly what he wrote; I just remember thinking Norm was working hard to tell a story, a real story. Sometimes I had a hard time following where his brain was going; it could have been him or me, I don't know. In the end I felt honored that he trusted me enough and valued my feedback that he shared his writing with me. I think that's the point: to respect him and his work. My opinion is worth what you pay for it, as they say.

Most stalwart volunteer

Jerry is in his fifties and lives in a subsidized apartment building near the shelter at which we serve our daily breakfast. When I first met Jerry, he had a modest, part-time job at a local printing firm, but when the recession in 2008 hit, he lost his job. I know he struggles with some medical conditions, and I see him have small seizures from time to time. Even when you feel you know someone, if the information isn't volunteered, it can be awkward to ask. I guess I try to balance my concern for him with a respect for his privacy. I've asked him about his condition a few times, and he just indicates it's not serious and that he's okay. I find it difficult to know where to go in the conversation after that response. So we just simply keep an eye on Jerry, and if he seems to be struggling, we give him some space. There's not yet been an episode that seems to require medical attention. We'd dial 911 if that were the case.

Jerry is a very sweet and gentle guy. He's never been married and his extended family is local people with whom he has a connection. Our group of volunteers, a different clan that shows up every day, is a little bit like family to Jerry.

He's our most dedicated volunteer, the only person who serves this ministry 365 days per year. Jerry shows up when we're in the middle of meal preparation, steps in to serve when we're lacking help, and

The heart of the matter (serving)

most importantly handles the after-meal logistics of staging the carts for the next day's team. This is a really critical function because when volunteers show up at 4:30 a.m., they don't want to have to start packing up to move across the street to begin meal preparations. They just want to get moving. Jerry helps make that happen.

The important element Jerry adds to our teams is when he prays as we close each morning's serving. Let's say that Jerry is a rock star servant as far as I'm concerned. (I discuss Jerry in another chapter as well.)

Most of us feel good when we've had the opportunity to serve others. We remember that feeling, and when the opportunity presents itself, we step in again, perhaps because we desire to recapture that feeling. The homeless are no different. The opportunity to serve provides a temporary respite from present circumstances and bonds people together around a purpose.

Many of the homeless I know are just like me. They want that feeling, too.

✦ ✦ ✦

CHALLENGE   Next time you're serving others, try to engage the folks you serve in some way. Come up with a thing or two to do and see if you can draft a couple of people to help. This interaction will mean a lot to them, a great deal more than being served.

CHAPTER EIGHT

DON'T BRING ME DOWN

(not defined by circumstances)

Have you ever thought about your answer to the question you're often asked when introduced to someone: "So what do you do?" Most of us believe that is a vocationally oriented question, so we answer with what our job is and possibly the name of the company where we work. From that point on, let the judgment begin.

Let's be a little honest here. We size others up based on the information and observations we make about them. Okay, maybe you say you don't, but I do. I admit it. And this tendency of mine has gotten me in some trouble over my lifetime.

Part of my job as a member of the management team in my corporate career was to interview people. Prior to making a hiring decision, we brought the person in, sat face-to-face, and asked him or her a series of questions designed to reveal the "real person," while at the same time the candidate attempted to put on his or her best to win the position. At least that's the way many hiring processes seem to be designed. As I reread that sentence, I believe this to be true but it all seems a little silly.

So here was my problem.

A candidate would be scheduled for me to interview. I reviewed the position description, prepped my questions, and determined my sought-after responses—another way of saying "right answers"—then brought the candidate into my office to begin the interview. I would say it took about five minutes or less, and I had already sized up the candidate and determined whether I liked the person for the job we had available—or not.

Hmmm. So what was the rest of the interview for anyway? If I was that quick to make a judgment about a person, it seems I was really not being fair to him or her, or at the least, not using an effective process in choosing someone to hire. I tried to break myself of this habit for a long time and found that I was too judgmental and couldn't do it. What a dilemma. I had to seek a solution by looking at the problem in a totally different way.

I just let it go. That's right; I just allowed the conclusion, whatever it was, to come to me. I would make my determination to hire or not hire freely without inhibition rather than trying to throttle it. However, the big change I made was this: I began using the remaining part of the interview to determine whether I was wrong or right in my initial inclination about the person. Let's say I thought I really liked this person for the job. Following each question, I would test that conclusion and see if I still felt that way or if that person's stock was sinking in my view. If I didn't like the candidate, I continued to ask my questions and try to visualize that person in the job. How would he or she interact with others on the team? How about handling pressure situations? Is my mind beginning to change about my

Don't bring me down (not defined by circumstances)

initial conclusion, or am I becoming more confirmed that I should pass on this person?

In order to do this, I needed to make one change that was difficult, but not as hard as trying not to judge. I had to suspend the need to be right. I like to be right. Don't we all? I like to think that I know the answers—I'm intelligent and experienced and I always come to the best possible conclusions. Always. As I consider that last statement it begins to become easier for me to see that it's not true. I'm not always right, my experience sometimes isn't enough to bring me to the best answer, and even my intelligence lets me down from time to time. Once I let go of the need to be right and allowed my judgment of candidates to happen in my natural timing, I became a much better interviewer.

Do you think I came to the right conclusion?

I believe I came to a functional conclusion at the time, recognizing I'm not a perfect person. I am judgmental and, at least at that time, seemed unable to change that. So I did the next best thing, and that was to recognize the tendency in myself and leverage it as a strength.

Presumptions of people

There are problems with being judgmental. We draw conclusions about others without all the information. We lump people into classes based on a variety of characteristics then assume that our experiences, or worse yet our assumptions, of those people are the same as all others in the same category.

Young people with tattoos or piercings can't be taken seriously. A good-looking guy driving a BMW must be rich and have his life all together. A young man in an urban area with baggy pants wearing a backwards cap must be a gangbanger and a thug. And here's the thing—all of these "perspectives" are coming from our own perspective and life biases. If you're a member of one of the aforementioned groups, you may have your own biases about each of the other groups and of me: a white, middle-age suburban guy. It makes no difference. Each of the above judgments is wrong. Not because the judgment turns out to be wrong, because sometimes it is accurate. It's wrong because it's unfair to the person upon whom the judgment is rendered. He or she was not given the chance to be considered as an individual: a unique, creative, interesting, kind, or generous person. We just stamped a label on them.

I see this happening with the homeless all the time. And I've got to share with you that it hurts. It really hurts those upon whom the judgment is laid. They know it. They can tell by how we look at them or how we avoid looking at them. We speak differently, in a dismissive way that shows that we're bothered. We don't engage them, we walk around them, and we surely don't provide them with the free gift of our smile. No, they might want something from us if we do that.

Look, don't take the above paragraph as me judging you. I'm not. The above paragraph is *me* only a few years ago. But I would ask you to examine your own heart as you consider the above descriptions and be honest about your feelings. Who are you trying to fool anyway? And if you're like most people who have had candid conversations with me about how they feel about the homeless, you may find you align with the above more than you do not.

In spite of society at large placing judgment on people who are homeless, some of them refuse to accept the label.

Mom helping first-time mom in a homeless shelter

Carla got a call from a young woman, Lisa, who had recently had a baby girl, her first child. The shelter she was at provided a daily ration of baby wipes and diapers. She had no family in the area and was

Don't bring me down (not defined by circumstances)

feeling very alone. Someone gave her the phone number of our organization and she pleaded for help. Naturally, we agreed to step in to help her and her young child. Carla, an experienced mom, went shopping for the needed supplies. There was another client at the same shelter who also had needs to fulfill. Since Carla was busy meeting with yet another client, I agreed to deliver the baby items and meet the other client before heading off to another shelter for the evening.

That's when I met Deanna.

Deanna wasn't from the Twin Cities either. She was middle-age and had two teenage kids. She claimed to never have been without housing, and she and both her kids were quite upset that they were in a shelter. Embarrassed and shocked were words she used to describe her feelings. Deanna was working and had lost her housing due to some circumstances that she explained only in highlights.

Here's what I thought was cool. Deanna was very insistent, positive to the point of smiling, as she described how she was going to see to it that they made it out of the shelter. She had a plan, and within a few weeks she and her children were moving into a new place. She exhibited a level of optimism that I could only hope to have while being in a situation that seems to undo most people.

Even better was how Deanna handled things with Lisa. The lobby at this shelter has tight security and doesn't allow visitors through the turnstiles. So Deanna and I were relegated to having our meeting in a tight little corner of the lobby. I had several large bags to give to Lisa, and I figured she'd need help getting them up to where she was staying. That's why I had asked Deanna to come down to see me first. I was intending to ask her to help Lisa up to her floor with the items I brought.

When I asked this of Deanna, she beamed. Not only did she say, "Of course!" but also offered to hang around Lisa and her daughter during her stay to look after them. Two experienced mothers: one purchasing goods for the baby and the other helping to deliver the items and care for the mom during the remainder of her stay. It would have been easy for Deanna to lose hope or just focus on herself and her children's immediate needs. Instead, she remained hopeful, worked to move forward through her current housing dilemma, and had the heart to help another.

Deanna did move into the home she was working towards. And Lisa got an apartment with some assistance from our social ministry. She not only got a home, but a small army of volunteers rounded up all the items she needed to outfit her new apartment. She did have an appointment with another agency that was going to help her get some stuff for her place in a few weeks and at the cost of several hundred dollars for the fee and delivery. She canceled that appointment. It was no longer necessary.

Deanna and Lisa did not allow their circumstances to define them.

New scenery needed

I first met James at our daily breakfast outside a homeless shelter. He had moved to Minneapolis from another state to start a better life for himself. Never married, he lived off the generosity of relatives, especially his mother, for most of his adult life. James held a variety of modest jobs, but used the money for his own pleasure since he really didn't have the responsibility of needing to keep up with rent or other financial obligations. That was taken care of for him.

James shared with me that his mom, now in advancing years, had had a hard talk with him that he needed to go out and make it on his own. His other siblings had done so, and now it was time for him. She was concerned that if he continued to hang around where he grew up that the influences that dragged him down in the past would continue to do so. It was time for a geographic cure.

Don't bring me down (not defined by circumstances)

He believed that the Twin Cities had a better quality of life. The people were nice and the city was safe. Most important, there were jobs. And with the nation just now slowly waking up from its latest recession, going where the jobs were was critical.

Not all of what James learned about Minneapolis turned out to be true, at least not to the extent he had heard. Many of the people were nice, but there was a veiled animosity towards those "not from here." It seemed this disposition was even more prominent when one is an African American man with a limited education. Housing was expensive. He figured that nearly any modest full-time job would be enough so that one could rent an apartment, purchase a car, and pay for all else needed to live. Not so. Affordable housing in the Twin Cities is limited and without the aid of an agency or some form of a subsidy, it's really tough to make it on a limited budget. He also found that with a felony in his very distant past, he continued to get denied housing after completing the application and paying the application fee; once the background check came back he was turned down. This became so frustrating that he finally started to tell the landlords in advance about his felony, just to save the application fee. They simply told him that they couldn't move forward without the fee, so he'd pay it only to get the same result.

Finding work was another problem. The felony issue interfered with that, too. Minnesota has a law recently placed on the books that does not allow employers to ask about past criminal records until a conditional employment offer has been made.[1] So at least in one instance, I know James applied for work at a job fair for a prominent Minnesota manufacturer, passed the profile screening, interview, and skills testing only to be turned down with the return of the background check. For a manufacturing job no less. I share his frustration.

James has an indomitable spirit. I've seen him get down only to get back up and move forward again. He's tried a variety of different jobs and worked through temporary agencies with the hope of being hired on full time at a good company. Oftentimes he's been used for short-term assignments then let go when the work is complete. There's no way to get a permanent residence with such an inconsistent income.

As of late, he has found he really enjoys manufacturing, working with his hands and seeing the fruit of his labor. He tells me of how his new employer has plans to train him on new machines. The company he is with now had him on their payroll only to let him go when work got slow. After working a couple of other jobs, they since have called him back and seem to have the contracts necessary to keep him employed. Our social ministry has a great partner that has rooms for rent without requiring a background check. The rent is due weekly, which helps residents manage finances more effectively than having to come up with such a large amount at the first of the month. Budgeting money when living on little margin seems to be a common challenge. This place has a nice model that helps with that.

James continues to struggle with his finances and has surprises pop up from his past in terms of financial obligations that he must meet. I get frustrated with his lack of transparency with me at times, but I guess I really don't know what I'd do if I had things like that in my past. I don't know that I'd want to tell anybody about them either and probably would just hope they would go away. That seems to be James's primary means of dealing with those things. I don't like it, but I guess I can understand.

Is James a success story? Do we have a happy ending yet? Sometimes there's more yet to be written. In James's case, I'm sure there will be. And good or bad, whatever the case in his circumstances, we'll be there to support him.

Always seemed to be in trouble

When I think of someone who wasn't defined by his circumstances the apostle Paul jumps out at me.

Don't bring me down (not defined by circumstances)

You may have heard of this guy. He wrote a big chunk of the New Testament. I think of him as a rebel, a tough guy with an abundance of resolve. This is the kind of guy you want on your side when you're in trouble. Or in Paul's case, it seemed he found an awful lot of trouble himself.

During Paul's travels, his objective was to set up new churches all over the known world. He would write letters to those same churches providing further instructions, guidance, and encouragement. Often the letters were directed toward the church's leadership and sometimes at the congregation at large. Paul's typical mode of operation would be to arrive at a location where he felt moved to share the Good News about Jesus, start to develop leadership, and birth a new church. After some time, many months and often a few years, Paul would move on to the next location.

Sometime after his departure, someone would communicate with Paul, who was now on to a new chapter in his church planting life, and update him on how the new church community was doing and what challenges they had. I can only imagine Paul's frustration, as it seems that these groups would get away from the central message of the Gospel and become distracted by a variety of things, or they'd become discouraged. So rather than traveling back to the church that needed direction, Paul wrote a letter that would be delivered to the church leadership. These same letters make up a large part of the New Testament.

When Paul wrote to the Philippian church, he seemed to be grateful for their support and wanted to thank and encourage them. But here's the catch. At the time Paul was expressing his heartfelt thanks for all the financial support they had provided him to plant new churches, Paul was imprisoned in a Roman jail. I'm not sure this was like a cakewalk for Paul, but considering all the other trauma he experienced during his missionary journeys, this might have been one of the least awful circumstances. It's almost too much to believe, but Paul had been beaten with whips and rods, stoned nearly to death (old-school stoned, not like the present!), shipwrecked, bitten by a snake, and put in jail more than once. Paul was a guy who understood hardship. And Paul was a guy that didn't let his circumstances get him down.

Just imagine all that Paul had been through while you read the following passage: "I know how to live on almost nothing or with everything. I have learned the secret of living in every situation, whether it is with a full stomach or empty, with plenty or little. For I can do everything through Christ, who gives me the strength" (Philippians 4:12–13, NLT).

Wow. All I can say is "wow." Knowing all that we know about Paul and his struggles, it is clear that he found a way to rise above them and remain other-focused, rather than on his present situation. I see that lived out regularly with the homeless.

We don't pick our parents

My friend Michael did not allow his circumstances to define him either. Growing up in a downtrodden area of the city he's from, his mother had several children with more than one father. Michael lived with his mom and step dad and had only an occasional relationship with his father. That father, with whom Michael fantasized about having a relationship, broke promise after promise to connect with Michael. For his birthday one year in his early teens, Michael's father took him to a place where he picked up some women. They drove for a while and parked in a discreet location. One woman sat in the front seat and the other in the back with Michael. To Michael's amazement, the women were prostitutes, and this was the "gift" his dad provided for his birthday. After the encounter, that evening Michael began to notice some problems in his lower region. Too embarrassed to tell anyone, he tried to keep it to himself until finally he told his dad about it. His dad laughed and brought him to a doctor, a friend of his father's,

Don't bring me down (not defined by circumstances)

and they both had a good laugh at Michael's expense. Michael tells of another episode when his dad was shooting at him while Michael was chasing after his dad in his car, trying to catch up to him. Yes, shooting. His father was shooting a pistol at his own son. Some father.

Michael got tangled up in the local drug scene, spent time in juvenile detention, and ultimately graduated to prison in his early adulthood. It was during his time in prison that the lightbulb went off. Or maybe it was something else. It's a long and very interesting story, but I'll sum it up by jumping ahead to Michael's thirst for God's Word through Scripture. By means Michael cannot explain to this day, he was allowed in the hour or so before dawn to leave his cell and head to the basement where sat a single chair. He would pull the chair over to the furthest back corner of the room, read his Bible, and pray. In that place, Michael's heart was transformed—in a prison basement no less.

After prison, he was taken in and mentored by a couple, and he helped with their church. In need of a fresh start, Michael came to Minneapolis with only a few dollars in his pocket and a suitcase that held all his earthly belongings. He wanted to enter a program he knew about that had the reputation of restoring lives in people who had done all they could in the past to destroy them.

I met Michael when he worked security at a homeless shelter as he was finishing the program. Michael was kind, patient, and helpful to all the clients he handled. Understand that being kind, patient, and helpful can be a tall order when dealing with people who are displaced from their homes for a variety of reasons, and in the wee hours of the morning, the place can get a little crazy. Michael was a soothing balm at that shelter, always calmly and quietly bringing order to every situation. It also helps that he's built like a freight train.

Now he's full-time on staff at the same shelter that housed him after stepping off the bus several years ago. He's married to a great woman and has the opportunity as part of his job to minister to those young men (and women) who are presently stuck in the same circumstance in which he found himself. He didn't want to be there. He didn't know anything else. And without the love and guidance of a few people as well as a belief in a Lord that takes in all comers, no matter their past, this story seems certain for a different ending. It makes me wonder how many other of our youth would turn around when given the same opportunities as Michael.

Suppose you're wrong

I began this chapter on what may seem a thread of being judgmental. Okay, well I did. But it's related to the idea that people do not need to be defined by their circumstances. When we place judgment on others, it creates a force like a gravitational pull on the person being judged to be drawn towards the judgment. For example, if you see someone who looks like a reckless youth with tattoos and piercings, you contemplate all that you believe is true of "those people," and based on your behaviors and thoughts, project your belief onto that person. Sure, some people are capable of choosing not to accept what you project. But it's a very subtle thing, kind of under the radar. And when person after person after person acts the same way, well, it seems that it must be true. It's hard for the judged person to escape it.

As a society, we assume a seemingly unclean, backpack-wearing, shuffle-as-they-walk person in an urban area or the prototypical cardboard-sign-holding guy or gal at the intersection is likely homeless. That means certain things to us. It means there might be a drinking or chemical dependency issue. There is also the possibility of mental illness. It may be a person who is lazy and doesn't want to work. In any case, it's likely a combination of those factors. And either way, we're not going to get involved.

Don't bring me down (not defined by circumstances)

This chapter highlights a few of the people I have found to be remarkable and who have risen above their circumstances. Circumstances that they didn't necessarily create, but truth be told at various points in their lives they may have contributed to their staying in their downtrodden state. In each case, someone believed in each of these people. That person took the time to know them, instill hope in them, and reach out and offer aid when it was needed most. Is this a formula to "fix" all the people in society we might consider broken? What would be the success ratio if we did this throughout our cities and neighborhoods?

I don't know. People are complicated and not in every case does someone make a radical transformation. But consider this. If you were that one person who was at a low point in life, you've had some rough circumstances and you know that your station in life is evident to all around you. How would you feel about one person agreeing to love you right where you're at? Would you respond in a positive and proactive manner in your life if you felt that you had someone in your corner? We seem to think of those people as statistics. But one person matters. And if all we do is make the difference to one, don't you think it matters to that one?

In the parable of the lost sheep, Jesus offered this challenge to the religious people of his time through a story: "If a man has a hundred sheep and one of them gets lost, what will he do? Won't he leave the ninety-nine in the wilderness and go to search for the one that is lost until he finds it?" (Luke 15:4–5, NLT).

One matters. It matters everything to the one who is the recipient of grace, generosity, and kindness.

● ● ●

CHALLENGE Push back on your old paradigm and suspend your judgment on the homeless. They might have more education than you, have people that love them, have children that miss them, and have a heart that is broken and in need of repair by a stranger who offers a kind word, a smile, and a small gift of money, socks, or a gift card.

CHAPTER NINE

IT'S BETTER TO GIVE

(generosity)

Most people think they are generous. In response to the question: "Are you a generous person?" I believe most people would reply, "Well, I certainly could do more, but generally yes, I am generous. I give to this and that, and I do my best to contribute to various causes. Like I said, I could do more, but sure, I give."

Statistics tell a different story. I found a variety of sources that tell in general, Americans give between roughly 2 or 3 percent of their income to charity.[1] That's it. About two or three cents out of every dollar or about $1,000 dollars for a family income of $50,000 per year is given away on average. If the average price of a latte at your favorite coffee shop is about $4, having one each day on the way to work is about the same amount: $1,000 per year. So why don't we give up our lattes and give more to those in need?

THOSE PEOPLE

An interesting aside is that one of the data sources in which I discovered the statistics on giving is an organization called The Philanthropy Roundtable. Their stated mission is "to foster excellence in philanthropy, to protect philanthropic freedom, to assist donors in achieving their philanthropic intent, and to help donors advance liberty, opportunity, and personal responsibility in America and abroad."[2] Sounds like reasonably good intent. What I really found interesting is that they have several meetings around the country each year for their membership at various locations, such as the Ritz-Carlton in Arlington, Virginia, the Princess Hotel in Scottsdale, Arizona, and The Breakers in Palm Beach, Florida. I guess people doing the serious work of philanthropy must find it necessary to meet in seriously nice places. Yeah, sarcasm. There may indeed be some reason for it that I don't understand; it just doesn't look good.

Make more ... take more

I would suppose that as we move on through life, get promoted, change jobs, and continue to develop our careers, we find we have the opportunity to give more financially. As one's income increases it stands to reason that we have more free cash flow from which to give. This is hardly the case. Most research indicates that as we earn more, we spend more, mostly on ourselves. And there is a strange anomaly in the data. All income brackets give the same 2 or 3 percent of family income to charity other than the lowest earners. Families earning between $25,000–50,000 per year give an average of 5 percent of their incomes to charity. More startling is that families with incomes less than $25,000 give a whopping 12 percent to charity on average. The report provides an explanation that those who are "religious" may tithe or otherwise give generously, even though their means are modest. Another suggestion is that the elderly that tend to have little or no debt may have the means to give more.[3]

It's better to give (generosity)

What seems odd to me is that we certainly have religious people who make more than $25,000 per year, so why is their giving not moving the needle on overall giving for their income bracket? How about debt? Are we so seriously in debt all of our lives that we can't seem to believe we have the means to give more?

I think this is how the American dream fails us. In our pursuit to continue to upgrade our lives, we improve our homes, trade in our vehicles for the latest model, and keep up with technology by updating our mobile phones every two years. Somehow we're led to believe that if we keep improving our stuff, we'll feel better because we've "made it." Sadly and oftentimes this is done through the use of debt, so we really don't own the stuff we bought. It owns us.

In our consumer-driven economy, we're marketed to continuously. We drive by billboards, and see ads on television, our computers, and our mobile phones. And most modern marketing isn't about touting the benefits of the product, but it's about creating a sense of dissatisfaction in us. We watch a commercial starring physically attractive people, in the middle of their workout at a health club, showing off their lean physiques, running and sweating, and then at the end we see it's a commercial for beer. Really? What's the message? If I drink that beer I'll look like that and so will all the people I hang out with? It totally doesn't make any sense but somehow we buy into it. Our need to be accepted or loved is so great that we'll even accept the nonsensical plot of a beer commercial.

The messaging is simple. Your stuff is out of date. Your car doesn't have the newest technology. Your phone is a model six, and now the model seven is out and does things the model six can't. I could buy this machine or work-out video and look like the people in the commercial. Or better yet, I could go to a clinic and get liposuction that would be so much easier because I wouldn't have to wait for the results. You are out of date, obsolete, and behind the curve. And other people are not. So which would you like to be?

THOSE PEOPLE

The hole we have inside of each of us that longs to be loved and belong is a deep crevasse that leads to a bottomless pit.

Want to have a nice car?

I tend to drive older cars now, but earlier in my adult life that wasn't the case. I had a "system," as I called it. I would purchase a vehicle that was about one- to two-years old, drive it for two or three years until it needed to have new tires and brakes installed, and then trade it for another one- to two-year-old car. My theory was that I was saving money by not putting tires and brakes into my vehicles while driving the latest model without paying full price. Since the cars I bought were just slightly used, I didn't have to absorb the initial depreciation that one has when purchasing a new car then selling it after only a few years of use.

I'm not here to tell you that was a bad system. As a matter of fact, there is some logic to it. Always have a newer, reliable, late model car in which you experience little to no maintenance costs. It wasn't so much that there was a problem with my scheme as there was an issue with my heart. My true motivation was to always have a "new" car, meaning one that looked as though it was new. I wanted people to see that I was always driving the latest model vehicle. I wanted to feel successful, which meant to me that I needed to believe others saw me as successful. To that end, I would study the model years of the new vehicles coming out and always try to purchase one on which the manufacturer had just recently updated that model's exterior aesthetics. Automakers only make major changes to the exterior look of any given car model every three or four years. It's too expensive to do it more often. So if this is the year a new look on my selected model comes out, I would plan to purchase that model the next year. Then I save on the depreciation, the car looks like the latest model, and it will continue to look "new" until I trade it in two or three years later.

It's better to give (generosity)

As I contemplate all this now it seems so silly and self-centered. I did not have the self-awareness then to understand what I was doing and why. It all seemed to be for a logical and well-intended purpose. And in no way is this an indictment of those who purchase and drive newer cars or upgrade any other stuff. This is a personal matter. It is a matter of the heart. My aim in dragging you through my retrospective thinking on car purchases is to provide an example of how we might be more thoughtful in our consumption habits and be totally honest with ourselves about why we do what we do.

Here's an epilogue to the car-buying story. I have a serious struggle with ego and humility. I have my entire life. Meaning I have too much ego and not enough humility. I admire those I see who are humble, and I have desired to become humble as well. I'm not sure it's something one can work on, but I do think there are things I can do to prevent my ego from being a dominating force in my life. The car I drive currently is an outdated model, actually not even in production any longer. The rocker panel on the driver's side is nearly completely gone due to rust. The black paint has a number of scuffs and witness marks from the various attempts to touch up the blemishes. The front sidelight on the passenger side was missing a lens until I fashioned one from a cutout piece of a windshield wash jug. It has low miles for its age, it runs well, and most of the features on the car still work.

It's hard to have a big ego driving this car.

My car buying system could have continued to steal away the joy and satisfaction of knowing that God is working in me to shape me into the image of his Son. Jesus exemplified humility. I want that for myself: to be more humble. For me, I had to drop the car-buying scheme to allow God to begin to work in my heart and start to change what I valued. As usual, a key part of my role in this is to get out of God's way and let him work in me.

THOSE PEOPLE

Why be generous?

Here's a cool thing about generosity and God's stand on it. He commands us to give and be generous. Not only is this required of us, but God explains the benefits of giving to us. I found about seventy verses in Scripture that address the subject, and I'm sure there are many more depending on how one searches.

Early in recorded human history, God provided direction to the Israelites on how to maintain healthy lifestyles as well as how to honor him. The book of Leviticus provides instructions on how to prepare various types of offerings and how to deal with certain kinds of diseases and physical conditions as well as proper sexual practices. Even in an agricultural-based economy, God determined it was important to give. Throughout human history, there have been people who were poor and in need of community support. So God directed those in charge of the crop harvest to not harvest from the edges of the field and to also leave behind whatever crops were dropped to the ground during the process. The landowner was to leave this behind for the poor so that they could gather the left behind crops for their own consumption. This process was called "gleaning." Even without the benefit of having currency, a banking system, or 501c3 charity status, God set up a means for people to give as well as a system to feed the poor.

John the Baptist came to prepare the way for Jesus to begin his earthly ministry. John preached a message of repentance, or said another way, a message of change by people turning around from how they were living to live in alignment with God's will and character. During his first recorded sermon to his audience, John was raining down fire and brimstone on the crowd, calling them a "brood of snakes" (Luke 3:7, NLT) among other things. After the tongue lashing, the question was asked of John: "What should we do?" John provided direction on several forms of conduct that should be changed. The first among these was to be generous. "If you have two shirts, give

It's better to give (generosity)

one to the poor. If you have food, share it with those who are hungry," said John (Luke 3:10–11, NLT). God used John to convey his message that people loosen the grip they had on their possessions and to give from what they had.

But God didn't stop at issuing rules. He outlined the clear and desirable benefits of being generous.

We've all heard that it is more blessed to give than to receive. The apostle Paul quoted Jesus as saying that (see Acts 20:35). But here's something else Jesus said that is almost too good to be true, nevertheless guaranteed.

Speaking to the crowd, Jesus turned to the subject about giving (see Luke 6:38). He explained that what we give will be returned to us in whatever measure we choose to give. So the return of the gift, or blessing, is really up to us. If we want a great deal of blessing and gifts from God, we simply give more and he'll return more to us. If we're okay with a small return on the gift, then we give less. God leaves it up to us. We trust him, give, and then he gives back to us in the same measure.

Segue, here. Let's not go down the path thinking: If I give a certain amount away, I would expect that God will urge my boss to give me a raise the following Monday for a like amount. Or that if I express my generosity, I will be able to receive the same through the scratch-off on the lottery ticket I just purchased. I would not totally rule out those things, but that's the wrong thinking. God doesn't think like us, and he certainly doesn't value things in the way we do. In the earlier story about the tight grip I had on automobiles, I must say that I feel that I am so much better off now than I was when I was in the middle of that. Sure, I always had fairly new cars. To go along with that, I also had anxiety over financial issues and concerns about whether my vehicle was going to get scratched in a parking lot. Even better, others are beginning to see me as the vision I had for myself—conforming to the image of Christ as his humble servant.

So God commands us and he blesses us in generosity. But this overlooks perhaps the most important reason and effect of our giving.

Don't miss the most important reason

In Matthew 25, Jesus gives a pointed account of the Final Judgment. All people will be separated and put at either the right hand or the left hand of the Father. Then he will say to those on the right, "For I was hungry, and you fed me. I was thirsty, and you gave me a drink. I was a stranger, and you invited me into your home. I was naked, and you gave me clothing. I was sick, and you cared for me. I was in prison, and you visited me" (vv. 35–36, NLT). Then he said that the "righteous ones" will ask when did they ever see him hungry, naked, sick or in prison. And the response by the King? He said when they did these things to "the least of these" they were doing it to him.

Wow. Did you get that? Jesus says that when we serve others in need—those who are poor, lack housing, in need of basic necessities, or unable to meet their own temporal needs—we are serving the Lord Jesus. Whatever we do, however we respond, we are doing and responding as if directly to Jesus. I know the following example isn't possible, as God has no needs, but grant me some latitude. I can't imagine anyone who would meet Jesus face-to-face and see that he was in need of something, who wouldn't rush to his aid and throw aside all other things in that moment to help the one who sacrificed and suffered so much for us. Who won't do that? Yet how easy it is to get sucked into our busy lives and pass up on the opportunity to help others in need?

Jonathan Edwards, the great eighteenth-century American pastor and theologian, often preached on serving the poor. I love this quote of his: "We can't express our love to God by doing anything that is

It's better to give (generosity)

profitable to God; God would therefore have us do it in those things that are profitable to our neighbors, whom he has constituted his receivers."[4] God knows we need to give. He wired that into our DNA. He knows it's good and healthy for us to give and to worship him with our gifts. The problem is that God is fully self-sufficient and not in need of anything. So he designated others to be the recipients of those gifts that we desire to give to him. There are people who have needs and people who have the need to give and worship God. He set up the whole balanced system so we can give, honor him, and meet the needs of others directly. It's God's system. It's perfect.

Given by the least of these

I am astounded at the radical generosity I see at homeless shelters. It is common to see someone give up the last sandwich available or bowl of oatmeal to another guest waiting in line. I see generosity in action on a regular basis as I serve and observe the behaviors of our guests. These are some awesome people.

When I think of the giving by those who seem to have little, I think of two situations that had an impact on me.

I was in a men's shelter that I visit on weekday evenings. There's no formal plan for what I do there. Our social ministry provides towels and personal care products for the residents, and we have also put on a few barbeques for the folks to enjoy. I usually show up around 6:30 in the evening, greet the staff, and see if there's a need that we can fill. After that, I wander around checking in with my friends and meeting new people. I often end up in conversations that range from how the local sports teams are performing to prayer requests for a family member. It's always interesting to me how often the subject turns into a conversation about faith.

I also try to be sensitive to individual needs. With more than two hundred men on two floors in the building, it would be really difficult to meet with each person one-on-one and discover what his needs are. There just doesn't seem to be time. So I restrict my conversations to those men already known to me and anyone else who approaches or engages me.

Socks anyone?

One evening a gentleman asked if I had any socks with me. Apparently my reputation for supplying socks had preceded me. At most events and volunteer opportunities that support the homeless, I provide socks. I didn't identify the specific need myself. It wasn't my idea and was suggested to me by a homeless person not long after I started serving. This person shared that there are places at which they can receive socks, but there never seem to be enough. And some of the socks are recycled. Folks are sometimes suspicious that if the socks had been worn by someone else, they may not have been laundered before they were donated to another person. So fresh new socks are preferred.

Socks are a great way to meet people and engage in conversation. I try to use it as a reason to ask for a name. Then I repeat the person's name and pray for that person by name when I drive away. I'm not really good at it, but I work to try to remember names.

When I hand someone a pair of socks, I look him or her in the eye. Our eyes act as a lamp into the body providing light to the whole person. The look in the eyes often is a giveaway to how that person is feeling. And a light often shines in a person's eyes when his or her spirits are high versus the look in the eyes of a downtrodden individual. When I see that lowly look, I try to find time to return later to that person and ask how he or she is doing. The person may feel like sharing, or maybe not. But I try to make time to ask the question. I think it's important to care and to live that out by attempting to engage people.

It's better to give (generosity)

I do carry socks with me whenever I drive into the city, so I did have socks this particular evening. I asked the fellow for his name and his assigned bunk number. I told him I'd head out to my vehicle when I finished my other conversations in the shelter to grab a pair of socks that I would deliver to him. He was thankful and agreed with the plan.

There are people I've met in homeless shelters who really pick up *my* spirits. One of them is my friend Booker. Booker was less than a year out from losing his apartment; the full circumstances were unclear to me, and he was working diligently and patiently with a housing case manager to find a new apartment. The shelter life was wearing on him, and he let me know about it one evening. We had a long conversation. Booker is better at memorizing and quoting the Bible than I am, and he was sharing Scripture with me that gave him some hope and endurance. As we were hugging and delivering our parting words to each other, I shared that I need to run outside and fetch a pair of socks for another resident. That's when the graciousness of my friend Booker kicked in.

He asked me to wait a moment. He had a bag on his neatly organized bunk. He plucked from the top of the bag a brand new pair of high-end, wool-blend socks, the kind of socks people wear camping or hunting. The socks I normally give out, although new and clean, are basic cotton socks. When worn continuously day after day, they last maybe a week. The socks Booker had probably sell for about $10 a pair. Mine can be purchased for about $.75. You get the picture; these were really nice socks.

Booker offered his socks to me and naturally I declined. I had plenty of inventory so I didn't need to take Booker's socks to meet this other guy's need. He protested and insisted I take the socks. I continued to push back but Booker was holding his ground. Then it hit me. Booker wanted to give. Perhaps he even felt he needed to give.

THOSE PEOPLE

Giving feels good and right

How do you feel when you give? It is more blessed to give than receive, remember? Booker knew that. And in his situation, living in a homeless shelter, having limited income, and having to carry around all of his worldly belongings day after day, he had limited opportunities to be blessed by God for being a giver. That's when it hit me. I was going to rob Booker from his blessing of being a giver if I didn't allow him to give. That hit me hard.

I relented. I tried my best to thank Booker for his generosity and told him how much I loved that he was willing to give such a valuable and precious gift to another man who wasn't known to him. I felt honored to play a small part in a story that God had already written about Booker and someone unknown to him who was about to receive his socks. Booker didn't want to be identified either. So when I gave the man the socks, I simply told him that another gentleman in the shelter knew of his need and wanted to share from what he had. I felt like I wanted him to know that the socks weren't my socks but were a gift from a fellow resident. Gracious, generous, and in touch with God's promises. That's my friend Booker.

I recognize that you may think that giving up a pair of socks, even for a homeless guy, isn't that big of a deal. Maybe or maybe not. I guess it's not really for us to determine. Booker wanted to give and didn't know the identity of the recipient and wished to remain anonymous. I do believe that Booker was being generous.

Some people exercise radical generosity that most of us, including me, rarely exhibit.

Why is he living in a homeless shelter?

I've known Leo for about three or four years. He's a big, lumbering fellow who is easy to bring to a smile. He lives in a large homeless

It's better to give (generosity)

shelter in Minneapolis, and I met him during the daily breakfast that we serve there. The breakfast is served early in the morning, 5:30–6:30 a.m., and Leo attends because he works. Actually, he works two jobs and puts in fifty hours per week and sometimes more.

We have a bit of a kinship as he grew up in an area where I own a small lake cabin. I frequent his hometown often and even know the last names of some of the families with whom he's familiar. Finding common ground with people helps build on the relationship and provides an easy conversation opener. True in all walks of life.

I don't know why Leo lives in a homeless shelter. Sometimes I wonder things and don't ask. When asking a question, it's hard to sense if the answer is something the person does or does not wish to reveal. At one point early on after meeting Leo and learning about what a hard worker he is, I offered to connect him to a friend who has a rooming house with reasonable rental rates. Leo graciously accepted the information, but after I followed up with him a couple of times, I got the sense that he wasn't going to pursue it. This didn't make sense to me. If I were working that much I would want to move to a better place in the shelter that for a small fee provides a bunk, a locker, and three meals a day. Leo opts to live in the lowliest spot; he lives in the overnight shelter. Residents only get a bunk to sleep on, with no meal or locker. I don't get it and figured I never would.

Everyone loves a cute baby video

One Friday morning I was out on the street serving breakfast and I saw Leo. We exchanged greetings and got into our normal routine conversation about his hometown, when am I heading there next, and what he had planned for that day. As we were about to part company he said, "Hey, let me show you something on my phone. It's really amazing." Leo scrolled through his texts until he found a brief video clip. It was only about six seconds. The video was of a small girl, really small, roughly a year old. She was running with her hands waving in the air and giggling. The clip was short so he played it a few times so we could enjoy it together.

"Isn't that amazing? She went right from crawling to running! She completely skipped walking and just started running." He went on to explain that she and the mother are Jamaican. He joked about how successful the Jamaican sprinters are and that he had told her mother that she was going to become the female Usain Bolt, the world record-holding Jamaican sprinter. Neat story, cute video, but I was confused. None of this fit together.

Leo is Caucasian and a native to Minnesota; his ancestors came from Scandinavia. The little girl, the Jamaican, was black. And she currently lived in Jamaica. I still was not getting the connection, even more confusing.

I asked Leo for more of the background, how had he come to know these people? He said he had lived with some Jamaicans who had resided in Minnesota for some time and had become friends with a number of them, including the young girl's mother. When she returned to her home country, she became pregnant and wasn't married. The woman shared with Leo that the baby's father had urged her to abort the baby and that she had given serious consideration to that. She had a very modest lifestyle and didn't see any way that becoming a single mother was going to work. She simply couldn't provide for this baby. That broke Leo's heart.

To the rescue

Leo told me he felt that all life was precious. He felt like we all have potential and that only God knows what he has planned for this little baby. That baby might become someone great and make an impact in this world, and that opportunity would be stolen away if the mother terminated the pregnancy. So Leo stepped in. He has been providing her money and promised her that he'd continue to help her and that she should feel secure about that. She could afford to keep the baby along with his financial help. So she agreed to trust Leo and had the baby girl.

And this wasn't the first time Leo had become involved to help financially. He told me a brief account of another family he helped that had a young boy who now has become a medical doctor in Jamaica. He said this with a bit of enthusiasm, as though he knew that without his willingness to step in, Jamaica might have one less doctor.

Wow. That seems to be totally ridiculous, reckless generosity.

Let's take the varnish off this. Is Leo being scammed? Could it be possible that he was seen as a soft target by these folks so they could get him to send them money after they returned to their home country? Yes, possible. But remember Leo lived with these people for a period of time. They helped and relied on each other while living in community. And even if this were a hoax, that doesn't change the fact that Leo is exercising generosity with reckless abandon. He believes he's giving to help others in a meaningful and impactful way. You see, when givers give, the givers' hearts are changed. The receiver only gets the tangible gift. The giver receives peace and joy that surpasses all understanding. Leo is joyful. Leo is at peace.

The truth is, I still don't fully understand why Leo chooses to live in a homeless shelter rather than upgrading his living circumstances. But I do know that he is a radical giver. Leo and Booker set the bar pretty high as far as I'm concerned. They are both givers. They understand that they are called to give, and that God will bless them in their giving in ways that are greater and higher than our ways. It's one thing to be generous; it's another to understand the "why" and the "what" of giving. Leo and Booker get why and give, and they get what God will do when they give.

❖ ❖ ❖

CHALLENGE   Are you ready to be a giver, someone who is wildly generous? Maybe not just now, but you might admire others that are. Think of a person(s) you know whom you consider generous. Meet for coffee or simply call and ask them how they got started and why they give as they do. Then, choose one thing to try that would be a sacrifice for you. Whether you decide to give away half of your next bonus, go on a foreign mission trip, or take an evening to volunteer at a homeless shelter, choose one thing and do it. Be open to where God takes you on this new journey.

CHAPTER TEN

THE GREATEST OF THESE

(love)

Greek is "greek" to me, mostly. I really don't know the language at all, but as I've learned to study the Bible more deeply, digging into what things mean, I've learned that the Greek language is much richer than my native English language in some ways.

Greek has multiple words for the word *love*. In English, we are forced to know the context of a word before we know what it means. If you say, "I love to do that," it would mean that you're expressing how you enjoy and gain pleasure from that activity. When you say, "I want to make love to you," from the context that implies that you are expressing your desire to engage in a sexual act with the person you're addressing. I know that last sentence sounds a bit clinical, but I was a little uncomfortable as I was writing it so that style took the edge off it for me. We may hear someone say, "I love you, man," which may mean love at least in the sense that we care about the other person or it may even be more about what they do for us. So love is complicated. At least in English.

For many Greek words, for example the word *love*, the context is contained within the word's definition. You can express all of those things about love in Greek, but often the word itself defines the type of love one is expressing.

Agape vs. philia

There's an exchange in the Bible between Jesus and the apostle Peter that really makes the point. After breakfast on the beach, the resurrected Jesus asked Peter a simple but pointed question. He asked, "Do you love me?" Peter replied, "Yes Lord, you know I love you" (John 21:15, NLT). Jesus asked the question three times, basically in what appears to be the same way. Peter, who was noted as getting a little upset at the continued questioning, answered affirmatively each time. As I've read this over the years, in English, I've thought this exchange to be a little odd. Why did Jesus continue to seemingly badger Peter about his love for him? Maybe Jesus didn't believe Peter? Or, as I've read in some Bible commentaries, maybe Jesus asked three times because Peter denied knowing Jesus after he was captured and executed, just as Jesus foretold? Either of those reasons could certainly be the case.

The most common words for love in Greek are *agape, eros, philia,* and *storge*.[1] Eros refers to the form of love that is sexual in nature. The root of the word *erotic* comes from *eros*. *Philia* was considered to be the love or friendship between people, or brotherly love. The city Philadelphia draws from this definition, as its motto is the city of brotherly love. *Storge* was a little-used term that meant parental love felt for one's children. Kind of an empathetic love that means if they hurt, the parent hurts.

The greatest of these (love)

Agape is the kind of love that can't be earned. It is the purest form of love. It is a love that would be considered unconditional. The closest we might come to giving *agape* love may be in the love of an infant. A baby hasn't screwed up anything (yet), so we just love babies as they are: innocent, cute, and vulnerable. As for screw-ups, we all resemble that name. We all have fallen short and have denied, ignored, and replaced God in our lives on a regular basis. Even though he created us and freely gave all that we have, we continue to mess up. So God, with his infinite capacity to love, loves us anyway. *Agape*.

When Jesus asked Peter the question the first two times, he asked "Peter, do you *agape* me?" Peter's response was most curious. He answered Jesus, "Yes Lord, you know I *phila* you." So you catch it now. Jesus was asking Peter if he had a love for Jesus that was unconditional, knew no bounds, and was everlasting and sacrificial. *Agape* love. So it would seem that Peter is holding back a bit. He's not yet at that place where he's ready to love Jesus with reckless abandon. That's what Jesus wants from Peter and each of us. Remember, Peter may not yet be over the fact that he denied knowing Jesus during his capture, torture, and execution. Perhaps he's more than a little embarrassed, which may be putting it mildly.

Here's the cool part. The third time Jesus asked the question, he exchanged the word *agape* for *philia*. "Peter," Jesus asked, "do you *philia* me?" Why did Jesus do that? There's no explanation in Scripture for this so we're left to work that out for ourselves. I like the idea that Jesus requested of Peter exactly what he wanted, *agape* love. After asking twice, Peter wasn't ready to go there yet. If you know anything of Peter later in this life, he had a major part in spreading the Good News throughout the known world as a totally reckless missionary. Legend has it that Peter's life ended through crucifixion just as did Jesus' life. In deference to Jesus, his Lord, he requested to be executed hanging upside down. He felt he wasn't worthy of dying in the same manner as his Savior.

THOSE PEOPLE

What I really love is the idea that the third time Jesus asked the question of Peter and swapped out the "love" word, is that Jesus may have been coming to meet Peter right where he was at the moment. Jesus didn't ask Peter why he didn't love him unconditionally: "Remember all that I've done for you? Say, just a short time ago I hung on a cross and died to pay the price for your sins, remember that? So, what's your hang up, Peter?" But Jesus didn't do that. Rather, he came to where Peter was. Peter wasn't yet ready to give up the *apage*-type love for Jesus. So Jesus' response (my take on it) was more like, "That's cool. You're not ready to commit to *agape* yet. I understand. It's okay. I'll accept your *philia* love for now. Don't worry about it, Peter. I know you'll come to love me more and more with time. Then we'll *agape* together."

I think Jesus does that for us today too. He doesn't place conditions on his love, and he accepts us for who we are and right where we are. Does this mean we can go out and screw up intentionally because we know it doesn't matter since we can always come back to him and he'll accept us? Well, let's just say that as we get to know Jesus better and the Holy Spirit begins to scrub out all the junk in us, our lives begin to change. Little by little we begin to have our lives conform to how Jesus would have us live. However, our improved lives are still wildly flawed, and wrecked with mistakes, screw-ups, curse words, lusting glances, white lies, and the list goes on. We'll not be completely cleaned up on this side of heaven. Yet Jesus continues to meet us right where we are. Broken, sinful, wretched yet redeemed, and righteous only because of him. *Agape* love.

A very real struggle

I watched my friend Felix express his love, *agape* love, with a group of men that he didn't know.

Felix is not a native to the United States. He grew up in a war-torn area of Africa and enlisted into fighting for his people as a small

The greatest of these (love)

child. Due to his high intelligence, he was granted a scholarship to study in America and received his degree in his early twenties. He worked in various jobs. Ironically, he worked as a case manager for a housing agency associated with a homeless shelter. Now, homeless himself and struggling with a physical disability that causes him great embarrassment at times, Felix lives in a homeless shelter. During the summer months, he prefers to camp out, which can be very dangerous, especially for an older, somewhat frail man. I worry about him.

The church I attend puts on an annual retreat for the men every spring. We travel to lake country in northern Minnesota where we fish, golf, zip line, shoot paintball guns and real guns along with sharing bunking quarters. There's always great programming designed to encourage vulnerability. The lessons are relevant to men, and I always leave with my life enriched by the experience.

Every year, we extend invitations to men that we feel could really use the break and would enjoy the time away but may not be able to afford it on their own. Some of these men are those we've met while serving breakfast in the ministry my church has called "2.4 Ministries." My friend Dave first started this ministry in 2008 and then others of us joined in.

A brief aside: 2.4 Ministries

Dave is part of the men's group I attend on Saturday mornings. I remember when he started coming. He had been divorced, struggled with relationships with his kids, and was looking for a church home. He's an understated guy. He doesn't always say much, but when he does, it's always worth hearing.

He became involved serving at a weekly pancake breakfast in a park in Minneapolis. I don't know that whole backstory, but I know that Dave was a faithful volunteer. When that ended, Dave still felt connected to the homeless community and that it was being underserved. That's how 2.4 Ministries began.

Dave won't take credit for the idea, but the Holy Spirit moved in him and urged him to serve those in need. He set up shop at the largest homeless shelter in Minneapolis and began cooking a daily breakfast, served from 5:30-6:30 a.m. Yes, daily. That's love.

Oh, and the name 2.4 Ministries? What does that mean? It comes from the biblical concept of tithing, or giving back to God the first 10 percent of what we have or earn. After all, it's all really his anyway, isn't it, so what's the big deal? The big deal is that most people who profess their faith in Jesus statistically don't give more than anyone else and the average is way less than 10 percent of one's earnings.[2] Look, if you're feeling like I'm reigning judgment down on you right now, please don't. I believe that giving is totally between God and the giver. We can never outgive God, and I have no idea how much "enough" is for anyone else other than myself. We spend our lives continually challenged to figure that out. God uses giving as a way to cultivate our heart, taking the focus off ourselves and placing it onto those in need. He also uses giving as a way to protect our hearts from turning to other gods (small "g") like materialism. God is completely self-sufficient. He doesn't need what we give. But he knows that we need to give.

Each day at 2.4 Ministries, volunteers show up at 4:30 a.m. to begin food preparation. The cooking and setup take most of an hour, so usually no later than 5:30 a.m. we're set up to serve. We serve until 6:30 a.m., break down our tables, wash the pots and coffee urns, and stage supplies for the next day's team. That takes until about 7:00 a.m., sometimes a little less. There are twenty-four hours in each day. To tithe 10 percent of your time each day would be about 2.4 hours. From 4:30-7:00 a.m. is a little more than 2.4 hours. Hence the name.

The greatest of these (love)

Gracious speech

Dave brought Felix to our men's retreat that year. I'm not sure how much Felix slept because he was so excited to be there and wandered around the camp day and night enjoying nature and the beauty of the lake and woods. I knew him well from my time serving at 2.4 Ministries. I also spend time at other homeless shelters in the Twin Cities, so when Felix moved around, it seemed he and I would always run into each other. So, it was nice for him that he had a couple of people at the retreat who were familiar to him.

At least that's how the retreat started. It moves me emotionally as I recall how well the other men treated Felix. He was just one of the guys. He was invited to tables during meals, asked to participate in activities, and was frequently in conversations with any number of the campers. To me, it didn't seem like Felix was a homeless guy that was a guest as some sort of benevolent action by our group; he was just one of the guys.

He felt that way, too.

The part of the retreat that I enjoy the most is Saturday night. It's like the perfect storm. Guys have been together for most of three days. We've played together, and shared meals, bunk quarters, and bathrooms. The speaker and lessons have been delivered and worked on by then. We're all tired and looking forward to going home the next day. It's the ideal setting for something guys struggle with—vulnerability. Like I said, the situation creates the perfect storm for guys being willing to be emotional, open, and vulnerable.

Previous retreats have brought forward some very interesting and emotion-charged situations. We've spontaneously decided to gather together to pray for healing for one of the campers dealing with a life-threatening condition. We've had testimonies from men that have been life changing for those men with the courage to get up in front of the group and bare their shortcomings. It seems there are always tears shed at this event. This year would not disappoint.

I was the MC for the event that year. I was made aware that Felix wanted a couple of minutes to get up in front of the men because he had something to say. No problem, I thought. I was a little concerned for Felix. He's a pretty reserved guy. I also know since his stroke he's a little embarrassed by his appearance and speech, which I have actually told him several times are both very normal to me. I just didn't want the event to end on a downer for him. I guess I felt a little protective of him. So he and I spoke about his message, and I tried to prepare him a little in terms of focusing on keeping his message simple and to the point for maximum impact with the men. Boy, he did. Actually, he nailed it.

It was a simple message. Thank you for accepting me. Thank you for helping me feel welcome. Thank you for loving me. Thank you.

Importance of eye contact

Felix explained his experience on the streets in Minneapolis. In the eyes of many of those who pass by him each day, he has several things going against him. He's black. He's from another country so he speaks with an accent. Oftentimes he's carrying a backpack, which by the way, is a dead give-a-way for not having permanent housing. And now, being somewhat disabled and disfigured from his stroke, his appearance is not distinguished in his mind. Felix said most of the time, he feels invisible to people. And being invisible hurts.

I think one of the simplest forms of humanity we can share with another person is eye contact. We give and get eye contact from lots of people throughout the course of a normal day. We are willing to give it and expect to get it as a simple sign of engagement and show of respect from each individual with whom we communicate. Okay,

The greatest of these (love)

our teenage children may be the exception to this. They may not give us eye contact during their mid-teens, but that actually is normal for them. And as a parent who has survived those years with several children, I'll assure you, it gets better. The eye contact will return.

I get eye contact from the person working the counter at a convenience store. I get eye contact from another driver who reaches a four-way stop intersection at the same time as I do. My wife and coworkers make eye contact with me regularly as does anyone who knows me. No matter how casual or brief the encounter I have with someone, we make eye contact.

Not so when you're homeless. Up until a few years ago, truth be told, I would rather not look at a homeless person. I didn't consciously process my reasoning at the time, but I would try not to look at them. As I consider this behavior now, I think there were a couple of reasons. First, I felt bad. I felt bad for people holding signs outside my car window as I'm waiting at the stoplight. What's their story? Why are they here? Where do they sleep at night? Do they really need the money, or are they scamming motorists out of pocket change? I guess my pity could have also been mixed with anger and resentment, if that's even possible. As I said, I never really processed my thoughts in the moment; I just tried to ignore them.

The other reason not to look at a homeless person is because I feel like I'm being judged, not by the panhandler, but maybe by myself, or maybe by God, I don't know. I guess it just brings up the whole question of whether I do enough for others. Do I give enough of my money away to those in need? Do I find my joy in things other than God and my relationships with other people? If I look at them are they going to expect something from me? Anyway, the whole judgment thing just makes me feel really bad about myself. So to avoid feeling pity, anger, or judgment, I would just look away. And I know I'm not that different than most. Unfortunately.

THOSE PEOPLE

Not invisible

I often get asked by people who know I spend time connecting with the homeless what they should do when they encounter a homeless person. The answers can be conditional based on the circumstances; however, one of the things that I encourage people to do is make eye contact. Time permitting, introduce yourself and extend your hand. That's a start. Are some people you encounter going to be a little rude or put off if you don't open your wallet and pull out a twenty for them? Yes. But all the time we deal with rude people who aren't homeless. How about someone cutting you off in traffic? Or butting in line at the grocery store? And let's not even get started on telemarketers. The point is that the homeless are people who have needs just like you and me. They have a need to have an identity, to be recognized as a person, and to be greeted and treated with respect. Sure, there are some that spoil it for the many. But let's not ignore the many because of the few.

Felix often feels invisible, like he doesn't exist or those in his company wish he didn't. Coupled with other matters that seem to stack against him in our society, it's tough to feel like you're a person of any worth. At least until this men's retreat.

Here's what I love about Felix. It would have been enough for most to enjoy the retreat, the company of all the guys, to feel part of the events, and be "one of the guys" for those few days. He didn't see that as enough. Felix felt it was important to express his gratitude, to thank the men who made him feel welcomed, and to share his feelings so that others might better understand the plight of the homeless. Even though he was the benefactor of all this love he received, he recognized that real love flows two ways. It flows in and flows out. It's not a one-way street. He was compelled to overcome his fear of speaking before a crowd, of his embarrassment about his disability, his self-consciousness about his appearance, and his humiliation over his living situation, to let the love not only flow to him but through him. Felix knows love. And he loved those men so much that even in the face of adversity, he directed the new love he just gained, back to those who gave it to him. That's real love. That's Felix. My friend, a real man who knows how to really love.

The story continues

A couple of years after the speech at the retreat, Felix still remained homeless and living in a Minneapolis shelter. He was approaching his seventieth birthday, and I had been concerned about his health. I felt as if I could see the homeless shelter system sucking the life out of my friend.

Felix receives Social Security, not a significant amount, but enough that in the right living situation it could create a sustainable existence. Another part of the backstory is that Felix has two high-school-age children who live with their mother. He is not obligated to do so, but Felix provides financial support to them. As I understand it, the children's mother hasn't worked very much in recent years, so there's been a significant financial strain on the family.

I began urging Felix to allow me to help him find a financially viable senior living location. He agreed. I made several phone calls and ultimately lined up an appointment at a very nice and affordable place. I took time off work, picked up Felix, and we visited the place, including a tour of one of the apartments. At the end of the meeting with the location's intake person, we received an application and agreed we'd return it the following week. I asked Felix in the meeting if he'd like me to help with the application and he declined. I also offered to bring him back to deliver the application; again he said "no." Felix insisted he would take care of this on his own, so I acquiesced.

Several weeks after Felix declined to turn in the application to the apartment complex, I became concerned. I urged him to do this, I offered to help him, and I pleaded with him that he must get out of the shelter system to take better care of himself. He continued to delay and said he would do it soon. Something was going on that I didn't understand; then it hit me.

I sat down with Felix at the shelter one evening and told him I wanted to run a scenario by him and ask him if he would tell me if I was correct. He agreed. I told him that I wondered if he was concerned that his kids' mother may not be able to provide for them and that if Felix moved into an apartment and began to pay rent, his financial ability, flexibility, and liquidity would diminish such that he may not be in a position to help them to the same extent as he was currently. The whole time I spoke to him, he looked down, as if he were ashamed. I asked him if I got it right. He nodded his head up and down slowly.

I felt so bad. Here I think I'm trying to help Felix and yet all I'm actually doing it interfering, putting pressure on him, and making him feel ashamed. I marveled at the sacrifice he was making for his children and questioned myself if I would be capable of the same. The answer, honestly, is that I don't know. I'd like to think that I would be willing to live an impoverished life, sleeping in homeless shelters, shuffling around in the cold each day trying to get out of the weather, and experiencing the even colder postures by those ignoring me as I wonder what each of them thinks of me while they ignore my existence. I'd like to think I'm capable of that much love. The truth is, I don't really know. I'm afraid to know the answer. Maybe I'm afraid of what it might cost me to find out?

I put my arm around Felix while we sat on his bunk in the shelter, and I told him I supported his decision. I told him that I would do anything possible to help him remain comfortable while he chose to stay in the homeless shelter system. And that at any point when or if he changed his mind and would like to find housing, I'll be his advocate and help him through the process.

The greatest of these (love)

Would you agree that we'd live in a better world if there were more people like Felix? Yet we seem to be inhibited from expressing love to others even when we feel it. I'm not talking about holding a door open for someone at the grocery store or running an errand for your spouse. Sure, these are nice things and are indeed a form of love. There is an element of sacrifice or giving that is involved. You enter the store moments after the person for which you held the door. Or you may have postponed or even missed a television show you enjoy by volunteering yourself for the errand. But I would suggest those are closer to a form of *philia* and not *agape* love. And just because the object of your "love" happens to be your spouse or child does not automatically make it an *agape* love expression.

I do not intend to draw a thin line between *philia* and *agape* and argue the point of how well we have loved another. I simply contend that *agape* is a wild, reckless love. Think of your own examples. If you're stuck in the middle as to which form of love it is, its likely *philia* love. *Agape* is so far out there, there's little chance you'll miss it.

✿ ✿ ✿

CHALLENGE   Select a person who you believe could use your encouragement. Pick someone who may be unlikely to expect to hear encouragement from you (I'm not totally ruling out spouses and children, but that is not who I have in mind). Email, text, or best of all phone them and say what you love about them and what a difference they've made in your life. If they ask why you're doing it, just tell them, "no reason; I just was thinking of you and I wanted you to know that." *Agape.*

CHAPTER ELEVEN

CONCLUSION

The joke about this book is: "This is the book everyone thought I was going to write."

My last book, *Amazed: Why the Humanity of Jesus Matters*, is a book on Christology, or the study of Jesus' humanity. I was on a journey to get to know Jesus, and it was suggested that I read through the Gospel texts in the Bible: the books of Matthew, Mark, Luke, and John. Jesus is alive as a *man* in these books, so reading them would allow me to read his quotes that were captured by the authors and to experience him in real-life form. I read these four books continually for about two years, and then as I often will do with an interesting topic, I thought I would read more about the subject by reading some other books. However, I struggled to find books on the subject that weren't written by a PhD. It seems that the examination of Jesus' "man-ness" isn't a popular subject. For me, it was a groundbreaking experience to get to know the man Jesus, and it helped me develop my relationship with the complete Jesus—both God and man.

THOSE PEOPLE

I tell you this because when the book was published, friends and acquaintances who know me and know about the work that I do with the homeless would say, "I heard you just published a book. What's it about?" So when I would begin to explain the concept of the humanness of Jesus, why that's God's really big idea, and why it matters, well, I would often get blank stares or comments like, "Oh, that's really interesting," meaning, it's really not.

So the joke about *Amazed* is that I didn't want to write a book; I just wanted to read a book on the subject, but it hadn't been written yet. Now, for those disappointed with my last effort, here is the book you thought I would write.

At the Simply Jesus Gathering in Denver, CO, in 2013, I heard Philip Yancey say: "You can't worship a homeless guy on Sunday and ignore one on Monday." When I contacted Yancey to find out the source of the quote, he actually said he got it from Shane Claiborne, best known for his book *The Irresistible Revolution*. In any event, that thought has permeated my brain ever since hearing it. When Jesus offered a parable on the Final Judgment, he suggested there are both sheep and goats. The goats ignored those in need. The really scary thing is that the goats were the "righteous" ones. They would have been the seemingly good, religious, law-abiding people. Yet they ignored the poor. Jesus then offered what is a famous line: "I tell you the truth, when you did it to one of the least of these my brothers and sisters, you were doing it to me!" (Matthew 25:40, NLT). We have a higher calling than simply being good people, rule-following people. Jesus calls us to be people who will serve, give to others, and love others who are struggling. And Jesus gave us a pathway to serve him saying that serving others is as if we're giving and doing to him directly. Cool.

It's hard to get up at 3:50 a.m., drive to a homeless shelter, prep and cook for an hour, serve a meal for an hour, clean up for thirty minutes, and then get on with one's day. And yet we have a couple dozen

Conclusion

volunteers who faithfully have done this every single week for the past ten years now. I watched relationships blossom, smiles and hugs exchanged, tears shed, and phone numbers swapped between our serving team and the clients at the shelter. We've seen many clients come and go over ten years. We often don't know what happens to someone once they stop attending our breakfast. We always hope for the best, but the truth is, it may not be. We've known of clients dying tragic deaths and even had two murders during our breakfast, not in our immediate area, but just down the block. Being homeless is a hard and dangerous life, and sometimes we are unfortunately reminded of this.

I've watched many lives changed on the part of the servers. The occasional act of service during the holidays makes one feel good about oneself as a contributing member of the community. But radical, sacrificial service in which one is significantly inconvenienced on an ongoing basis can be transformative. There are many ways to worship—attend church, study Scripture, pray, sing—and I believe service is a form of worship when we're of a common heart with God's desires. Our teams worship every week, some people more than once per week. It can be intense, draining, heartbreaking, nerve-racking, and totally worth every second spent. I am so impressed and incredibly humbled that we have so many people continue to serve in this important social ministry. "Thanks" is too small a word.

I added an appendix on dealing with panhandlers because this is such a common question for those who know of my involvement with the homeless. In no way do I consider myself an expert, but for whatever it's worth, I offer my thoughts and suggestions that might just be different enough from yours that you might consider taking on a new approach or attitude.

My hope is that as you have read this book your paradigms about the homeless and chronically poor may have shifted a bit. I predict that you'll still continue to need to push back against being judgmental, because I still must. If you choose to become part of a social ministry to serve others on a regular basis, I would be greatly honored to know this and would love to hear from you. I can be reached through my blog at www.richardbahr.com.

And lastly, I must humbly confess that I am the great benefactor from all this. My hope is that the time, effort, and funds Carla and I commit to helping the needs of the homeless and poor will make a difference in the lives of those we touch. But honestly, both of our lives have been profoundly impacted and changed for the better through our sacrificial service, our financial giving, our new friendships among those we have served, and from those professionals who do this good work on an ongoing basis, many of whom have dedicated their lives to helping others.

Through all of this, I believe the work of God's Holy Spirit has presided at every step of the way, always providing what we need, leveraging our resources of time and money, and continuing to inspire and encourage us just when we need it. The work can be hard, but God has continued to be faithful and sufficient for us and sustains us through all the trials.

ACKNOWLEDGMENTS

There are always so many folks to thank when it comes to the completion of a project, and writing and publishing a book is a significant project that requires a team of people to do it well.

When the rough draft was completed, I wanted to get feedback on the book, its format, organization, and the content. I selected a number of people who know me, know my heart, and also have a heart for those in need and asked them to read the manuscript and provide me with feedback. The team of Joshua Gamradt, Elise Haider, Rob Van Beusekom, and Andy Zucaro read and provided useful (and critical) commentary that I used to prepare the final manuscript before turning it over for editing. Thank you for your time, diligence, and your willingness to be open and honest with me.

Jessica Ess did a masterful job on the interior design of my last book and for this book did both the cover and interior designs. Thank you for capturing the spirit of what I hope to convey to the reader with your creative talents.

Susan Niemi actually agreed to sign up to manage this project and edit the manuscript, even after working with me on my previous book! I'm grateful for how she complements what might be my conversational style of writing with her ability to bring me up a readership level while not losing my voice. Thanks again for your partnership with me on this project.

THOSE PEOPLE

Our publisher, Bill Huff, is an inspiration in so many ways. In dealing with his personal health challenges and the grace with which he handles his new physical limitations, he exhibits to me what seems to be the infinite capacity with which God provides to deal with all things, good and otherwise. I'm very appreciative of your confidence in me in adding your endorsement of Huff Publishing to this work.

When first inspired to write this book, I was in the midst of wrapping up my previous book. Carla and I were sitting in the Java House, owned by Sara Peters, in Fort Myers, Florida, contemplating ideas for my next project. We spent several hours there during a rainy and what would normally be a disappointing spring break day in Florida, and before we left we had the title (Carla's idea) and a rough outline for the book's content. Sara was a most gracious host and allowed us to return and host a book-signing event for the last book outside her shop the following year. Having owned and operated a small business in my past, I appreciate Sara and the work and risk that go into the labor of love that is the store.

My wife and partner in many of my adventures, Carla, inspires and encourages me to pursue those "God whispers" that come from time to time, such as writing a book. I can't imagine a more supportive partner; she also is always my first test subject for anything I write. And the work she does to advance our efforts in our social ministry, Threshold to New Life, is amazing and inspiring. Enough said.

The staffs that work at homeless shelters have very difficult and sometimes dangerous jobs. The two shelters I frequent the most are the Catholic Charities Higher Ground Shelter and Salvation Army Harbor Light Shelter, both in Minneapolis. I do visit other shelters and campsites from time to time, but much of my time, both mornings and evenings, are spent in these two places. The staff and security teams have always been most gracious and welcoming to me, allowing me access to the facilities and to sit with, counsel, encourage,

Acknowledgments

pray, or just simply hang out with the men who are overnight residents. I have so much respect for what you do. Thank you.

And finally, for those who continue to struggle with homelessness or are on the verge of homelessness due to a variety of circumstances: You have taught me, inspired me, loved me, and encouraged me, which would be what I would have expected to do for you. I simply did not expect when I began ten years ago that you had anything to give me. I couldn't have been more wrong. "Thanks" isn't a big enough word. You have profoundly and permanently changed my life for the better.

APPENDIX

Thoughts on dealing with panhandlers

One of the questions I get asked most often is: "What's the right way to deal with someone panhandling?" This question implies a question that is intended but not asked: "Should I give someone panhandling cash or not?" Actually, some people have kept it real simple and just start with the second question. I'll start with some background information to set up these questions and then give you my thinking on the matter.

The term *panhandling* refers to people soliciting financial donations from passersby at a public location, either on a street, subway, sidewalk, or roadway. Other terms used are *beggars* or *someone is flying a sign*. The giving of "alms" is referred to in the Bible, so an almsman or almswoman is one who is the recipient of charity and mercy as it is dispensed by the giver.

There is a lot of biblical direction on caring for the poor and the accompanying responsibilities, if you're one to heed this direction. And if not, please continue reading, and I promise at the end of this section there will be practical direction I believe you'll find useful.

Here are a few Scripture verses from Proverbs, a book commonly looked to as a source of providing practical wisdom, that weighs in on this matter.

"Whoever oppresses a poor man insults his Maker, but he who is generous to the needy honors him" (Proverbs 14:31, ESV).

"Whoever is generous to the poor lends to the Lord, and he will repay him for his deed" (Proverbs 19:17, ESV).

"Whoever has a bountiful eye will be blessed, for he shares his bread with the poor" (Proverbs 22:9, ESV).

"A righteous man knows the rights of the poor; a wicked man does not understand such knowledge" (Proverbs 29:7, ESV).

Jesus spoke about the poor and how we're to give from the heart and not for recognition from other people. In Luke 11:40–42 he indicts the local religious leaders (the Pharisees) for giving and being phony about it. Another time when he was speaking to a wealthy young man who says he'll follow Jesus and just needs to be told what to do, the man's response when Jesus says sell everything and give the proceeds to the poor (see Luke 18) revealed that he loved his money more than the call to follow Jesus.

There is much more in the Bible about the poor. If you want to know more, simply perform an Internet search for something like "what the Bible says about the poor" and you'll have all you need.

Is it legal to panhandle?

The answer in most places is "no." In my home state of Minnesota, state statute 169.22, Subd. 2 from 2017 says: "No person shall stand on a roadway for the purpose of soliciting employment, business, or contributions from the occupant of any vehicle."[1]

I wonder if "soliciting . . . business" also applies when a retail store has a person out with a sandwich-board sign or the like, working street corners attempting to entice passersby to their establishment. I have no idea, but my first thought in reading the statute was does this law deny any other activity that goes on without enforcement?

Appendix

Actually, in many major cities the panhandling laws are not enforced regularly. There may be certain parts of town or whenever a major event occurs—think Super Bowl, Final 4, or a political convention—that with the law already on the books, those in charge selectively decide it is time to follow the law. I'm not actually suggesting this is a bad thing; it does allow panhandling at many locations and lots of cities most of the time. I'm simply pointing out the legal angle to the question and how it is actually enforced—which appears to be selective enforcement. In my area, there seems to be no prohibition on giving to a panhandler, but you might want to check your local laws to see how this is governed in your area.

Another subtext to the question about dealing with panhandlers is: "Don't some of them just use the money for drugs, alcohol, or cigarettes?"

My answer is "yes." Some people do. And some don't. Are we morally obligated then to not give cash if the panhandler may spend it on such things? I'll come back to that shortly.

Here's another one: "I read that some panhandlers make a killing and actually live out in the suburbs making over $100,000 a year!"

My answer? Well, it is technically possible. If a panhandler solicited eight hours per day, six days per week, fifty-two weeks per year, he or she would have to pull down about forty dollars per hour. That would be receiving a donation at the rate of a dollar every ninety seconds. If the panhandler collects larger denominations of currency, the donations could happen less frequently. So like I said, it's technically possible. I've met hundreds of panhandlers in dozens of states around the United States and in several countries around the world. As for the local people in the Twin Cities, many of them I know by name or at least recognize them as a "regular." I haven't personally seen any evidence that a single panhandler lives far above the means he or she represents on the street corner. But like I said, it's technically possible.

THOSE PEOPLE

Back to what to do. I'd like to pivot here a bit to suggest that by asking the question, or by your interest in reading this part of the book, you have frequent enough encounters with panhandlers, and you have a genuine interest about knowing what to do. So thank you for your concern. My suggestion is that if you are reading this, you now have the responsibility to have a plan. From now on it is no longer acceptable for you to run into panhandlers and deny giving them anything because you don't feel good about it or you don't know what is right to give. When you have a plan, you're freed up to respond in what you've determined is a reasonable and appropriate way to help the person in need. Let's talk about elements of the plan.

As discussed earlier, there are panhandlers who are soliciting donations that will be used to purchase drugs, alcohol, or cigarettes. Should that be a problem with you? The question is less a moral question and more a personal one. One could determine that the giver is not accountable or responsible for how the gift is used. When I travel, and I'm not in my own vehicle, giving cash is the approach I use most often. Once given, you've done what you feel is right to aid the person and the choices become his or hers. I think this is a valid position. If you're not comfortable with that, let's move on to other strategies.

An approach I use most often in my local area is to keep a stash of socks and a few fast-food gift cards in the glove box of my vehicle. When I see a panhandler I stop, and I may choose one of the items to give or I may offer the panhandler a choice. In my case, I have a little message tract taped to the gift card ($5 value) and suggest he or she reads it while enjoying the meal. This steps up the accountability one notch, so that I'm giving something tangible and useful to the panhandler rather than currency. However, I do know there's a street value for gift cards and even for socks. So a desperate panhandler insisting on getting high may trade these items for cash, drugs, or cigarettes. It's not a perfect system.

Appendix

Another idea is taking a panhandler for a meal. This makes most sense when you're already on foot, as opposed to driving your vehicle. You can offer to take the person into a restaurant and purchase a meal. When I've done this and I have the time, I sit with the person and just enjoy the conversation. Based on the mental state of the panhandler, this can be very interesting. I would not recommend in most instances inviting a panhandler into your car. Stranger-Danger. The reasons not to do this are obvious. I've taken panhandlers not known to me into my vehicle but only on rare occasions.

Another way to respond to panhandlers that I've heard promoted is to give to a local charity. I'm not quite sure how to implement this, but maybe at the end of the week you could count the number of encounters you've had with panhandlers then give so much for each one. I guess I could be convinced this is a reasonable approach, but it does overlook one key aspect I have not yet discussed.

Not that many years ago, I would stop at a light in the city and try to look out of my left eye at the stoplight, turning my head and cranking my neck so that I didn't have to look at the panhandler just outside my window. I figured if I ignored that person, he or she would go away, and I wouldn't have to deal with the problem and hassle of panhandlers. People in homeless shelters have told me more than once how it feels to go through an entire day with every single person encountered attempting not to make eye contact with you. It's hurtful and inhumane. The least amount of dignity we can provide to another person is a look in the eye. Most of the panhandlers I talk to are humiliated about the act they are going through to obtain a few dollars and describe how hurtful some people can be by what they do and don't do.

I feel it's important to engage panhandlers. I ask his or her name and offer my name and oftentimes I reach for a handshake. I may ask, "How's this corner?" meaning how are the donations going. I may offer a "Be careful today" or "I hope you're able to get what you

THOSE PEOPLE

hope for today" or some little thing in an attempt to be encouraging during a traffic light stop that may be only thirty seconds or less. I've even been caught flat a few times when in another city with only credit cards and no cash. I remember one time in Tampa stopping to offer encouragement and apologizing, explaining that I was from out of town and had no cash and only credit cards. I was so sorry I had nothing to offer, but I offered my encouragement and hoped for his sake that he got his needs met that day. This particular panhandler was very gracious, said he understood, told me it was okay, and emphasized that he really appreciated having me stop and talk to him. Would he have rather gotten cash from me? Sure. But how uncommon is it to have someone stop and apologize for not having anything to give but well wishes and encouragement? He seemed genuine in his appreciation. Not all panhandlers are that gracious.

Another question is: "What if they (panhandlers) are rude or aggressive?"

At our daily breakfast ministry, if there's any kind of physical altercation, we shut down the breakfast immediately, dismiss all our guests, and throw away the food. Once we had such an incident within the first ten minutes of beginning to serve breakfast one summer morning, and it broke my heart to toss out all that food. The reason we do this is that we must not encourage poor behavior. There is a common decency and respect that people ought to have for one another. We want to reinforce this behavior and not reward (or allow) behaviors that are rude, threatening, or violent.

I believe the same applies to panhandlers. It has been a rare thing for me to encounter someone who is pushy or obnoxious, but it has happened. I've simply kept my window closed and allowed him or her to pass, or close it saying that perhaps another person would like to help, or something like that. I don't start an argument or attempt to moralize him or her. It may be the panhandler is under the influence of something that makes the lesson pointless anyway. I don't have great answers for these situations, except to say that in my experience, thankfully it doesn't happen often. There you go. Here's a recap.

- Make a decision about which approach you're most comfortable doing.
- Stock up on items (socks, gift cards, bus tokens, granola bars, water bottles, personal care kits, and so forth) and keep them handy in your car—or use cash if you're comfortable with that
- Make eye contact and greet warmly. Offer encouragement.

That's it. I'd love to hear from others on ideas and approaches to this. I don't have the corner on all wisdom that relates to this topic. You can reach me through my website at www.richardbahr.com and leave me your thoughts. With enough useful ideas, I could see turning this into a blog post.

Please remember, panhandlers are people.

NOTES

Chapter 2. Don't pray for this (patience)
1. http://www.merriam-webster.com/dictionary/patient
2. http://bibleornot.org/origin-of-patience-is-a-virtue/
3. http://www.biblestudytools.com/lexicons/greek/nas/hupomone.html

Chapter 3. What's the attitude? (gratitude)
1. A study cited by *Time* magazine advances a theory based on a study that a population's suicide rate increases due to our comparison to those around us, and it does so even at higher income levels, http://business.time.com/2012/11/08/why-suicides-are-more-common-in-richer-neighborhoods/
2. https://www.psychologytoday.com/basics/gratitude
   Janet Moore of the *Minneapolis Star Tribune* wrote a good article on the subject of the homeless and the use of mass transit as providing overnight shelter. Published in the January 9, 2017 edition.

Chapter 4. True grit (perseverance)
1. https://www.usda.gov/oce/foodwaste/faqs.htm
2. We were first introduced to the concept of contrasting relief and restoration as the aim of social ministry in the book *When Helping Hurts* by Steve Corbett and Brian Fikkert. For those working in a social ministry setting and especially those charged with making decisions around programming and the use of scarce resources, this is recommended reading.

Chapter 5. More powerful than a locomotive (stamina)
1. The average American only walks about half the recommended amount of 10,000 steps daily, according to Catrine Tudor-Locke, director of the Walking Behavior Laboratory at Pennington Biomedical Research Center. Last year,

she told Live Science that the typical American takes about 5,900 steps a day. http://www.attn.com/stories/2272/how-far-does-average-american-walk-day

2. Mayo Clinic's website defines plantar fasciitis http://www.mayoclinic.org/diseases-conditions/plantar-fasciitis/home/ovc-20268392

3. Project 6:8 is named for the Bible verse found in Micah 6:8 (NIV): "He has shown you, O mortal, what is good. And what does the Lord require of you? To act justly and to love mercy and to walk humbly with your God." Its website can be found at www.projectsixeight.com.

Chapter 6. You've got to have . . . (faith)

1. https://www.merriam-webster.com/dictionary/faith

2. https://en.wikiquote.org/wiki/Jesse_Ventura

3. Jim and Elisabeth Elliot led remarkable lives and several books have been written about their journey through faith and evangelism. My "cliff notes" were found at https://en.wikipedia.org/wiki/Jim_Elliot and https://en.wikipedia.org/wiki/Elisabeth_Elliot. A search by either name will provide other materials to read about their lives in more depth.

4. An extensive and impressive list of famous people of science that claim Christianity as their faith can be found at https://en.wikipedia.org/wiki/List_of_Christians_in_science_and_technology

5. For a more comprehensive study on homelessness in Minnesota, check out the Wilder Foundation's tri-annual report with the most recent data collected in October 2015. http://mnhomeless.org/minnesota-homeless-study/homelessness-in-minnesota.php#1-3457-g

6. This interpretation is found in John 14:26 in the King James Bible. In other versions, the same term is interpreted as *advocate*, *helper*, and *counselor*. The term used in the original Greek language was *paraclete*, meaning one called to the side of another.

Chapter 7. The heart of the matter (serving)

1. The Huffington Post article posted on the internet 2/21/2015 can be found at http://www.huffingtonpost.com/kathy-gottberg/volunteering7-reasons-why_b_6302770.html

2. http://kingjamesbibledictionary.com/StrongsNo/G1249/servant

3. http://biblehub.com/greek/1401.htm

Chapter 8. Don't bring me down (not defined by circumstances)

1. Minnesota statute 364.021 PUBLIC AND PRIVATE EMPLOYMENT; CONSIDERATION OF CRIMINAL RECORDS.

Notes

Chapter 9. It's better to give (generosity)

1. http://www.philanthropyroundtable.org/almanac/statistics/
2. Ibid.
3. Ibid.
4. Michael J. McClymond and Gerald R. McDermott, *The Theology of Jonathan Edwards* (New York: Oxford University Press, 2012), 518.

Chapter 10. The greatest of these (love)

1. https://en.wikipedia.org/wiki/Greek_words_for_love
2. http://www.philanthropyroundtable.org/almanac/statistics/

Appendix

1. https://www.revisor.mn.gov/statutes/?id=169.22

ABOUT THRESHOLD TO NEW LIFE

The social ministry Threshold to New Life (www.threshold2newlife.org) was founded in 2013 by Carla and Richard Bahr. Why do we call it a "social ministry"? Because we believe society and people (social) circumstances can be positively changed by our service (or ministry). Our aim is that our organization is "ministry" with a "social" aspect—ministry that affects and improves the circumstances of people.

In our first five years of operation, we have helped more than three hundred people and families maintain their housing—effectively keeping them from losing their housing. There is a large churn of the homeless obtaining housing then only to lose it again because they don't have the financial margin in their lives to deal with the unexpected things that come up. Our organization steps into the gap and helps those who need a little help.

Our most common circumstance is receiving a referral from one of our partner organizations, either a homeless shelter, a housing program, or a government agency, in which their client needs assistance but the help needed is beyond the referring agency's ability to help. We then assess the situation to try to determine that the circumstance is really only a "gap" in the person's financial life, and then provide a matching grant in which the client must come up with approximately one-half of the needed funds. These funds can be borrowed from friends or family, obtained from another organization, or may be repaid to the landlord over installments. We sometimes negotiate payment terms with landlords, and we put our funds in last and confirm with the landlord that the client's good financial standing has been restored.

Our average grant is three hundred dollars. Some statistics indicate it costs more than one hundred dollars per night to house a homeless person. So for about a three-day cost in a homeless shelter, we can keep someone from becoming homeless. We think our approach is cost effective, restores both the landlord and the client, and builds pride in the client as he or she actually participated in solving the problem. This is a humane, economical, and smart means of dealing with the problem.

Although housing and housing-related issues is our major focus, we continue to provide relief for the homeless in terms of clothing, food gift cards, bus tokens, and any variety of other things that help relieve a bit of the stress of the moment while giving us the opportunity to build relationships.

We use the image of a "threshold" as an illustration for the assistance provided. When one is standing at a threshold and takes one step forward, he or she is in a new place, albeit only one step away and in the next place or room. Threshold to New Life helps with taking the one, small step forward, and we hope with moving the individual into a new and better place.

ABOUT THE AUTHOR

RICHARD AND CARLA BAHR

Richard Bahr is a lifelong resident of Minnesota and grew up in the Twin Cities area. For twenty-one years he was president and partner in a successful firm developing packaging automation solutions for pharmaceutical and medical device firms.

Due to his own life experiences coupled with a passion for service, Bahr has been involved with organizations that provide a "second chance" to those in need. In 2013 he cofounded a social ministry with his wife, Carla, called Threshold to New Life. The organization's mission is to provide short-term relief to the homeless as well as to give assistance to those at risk of losing housing, effectively reducing homelessness. In 2017 alone, their organization played a part in preventing 146 people and families from becoming homeless.

Bahr has personally delivered more than 20,000 pairs of socks to his "friends" in the street as a means of meeting the homeless, learning their names, and establishing relationships. He spends evenings in homeless shelters, under bridges, and in camps, connecting with

About the author

people and encouraging and helping to meet the basic needs of "the least of these."

Bahr cofounded The Food Drive Challenge (now rebranded as www.corporationsfeeding america.org), which provides tools, tips, and techniques for business to conduct staff-driven food drives to support their local communities. He serves at and coordinates the volunteers for 2.4 Ministries, which provides a daily breakfast and fellowship at Minneapolis homeless shelter. He also volunteers at Project 6:8, providing a weekly, home-cooked meal under the I-394 bridge west of Dunwoody College.

He is a founding member of the Hennepin Technical College Foundation and served as its president for sixteen years, where he established the Bahr Family Endowment. In addition he serves as a mentor to chemically dependent men and has volunteered for Habitat for Humanity.

Bahr previously published the study guide for *Speaking of Jesus: The art of Not-evangelism* (book by Carl Medearis) and *Amazed: Why the Humanity of Jesus Matters*. All profits from his writing go to fund his social ministry work.

Learn more about Threshold to New Life and Richard Bahr at www.richardbahr.com.

Amazed: Why the Humanity of Jesus Matters

Released in 2016, this book examines the humanity of Jesus through the study of his "not so God-like" characteristics, such as weeping, exploding in an angry rage, being tempted to sin, praying, and even giving nicknames to close friends.

Why do these things matter?

When sin entered the world and separated us from God, God's plan all along had been to draw us back to him and into a loving relationship. How would God the Father do this? God knew that we would best relate to him if he were one of us. He's relational, and we're made in his image, so therefore we're relational. We can relate to, connect with, and ultimately fall into a loving relationship with God when we can draw close to him. God didn't need to come to earth as a man—*we* needed him to.

This book helps us connect with God through Jesus. Here's what readers have said.

> "I recommend this book to anyone wanting to get to know more about Jesus and prefers to have a thought-provoking conversation rather than lecture-styled teaching. No matter the question or problem, Jesus is the answer. I know we all would be helped greatly to take a page from the life of Richard, and keep our eyes focused on Jesus."

> "Rich does a great job outlining things about Jesus I haven't thought about before. He's engaging and raw about his own life and challenges. Well worth the read. Simple and fast for those who aren't theologians. Engaging in a way that challenged me to stop, think, and praise God for who he is and the life he lived and showed us."

Amazed: Why the Humanity of Jesus Matters is available online in paperback or as an e-book.

www.ingramcontent.com/pod-product-compliance
Lightning Source LLC
Chambersburg PA
CBHW030437010526
44118CB00011B/679